Jeremiah

INTERPRETATION
BIBLE STUDIES

Jeremiah

ROBERT R. LAHA JR.

WESTMINSTER
JOHN KNOX PRESS
LOUISVILLE · KENTUCKY

Book design by Drew Stevens
Cover design by Pam Poll
Cover illustration by Robert Stratton

First edition
Published by Westminster John Knox Press
Louisville, Kentucky

This book is printed on acid-free paper that meets the American National Standards Institute Z39.48 standard. ♾

PRINTED IN THE UNITED STATES OF AMERICA

05 06 07 08 09 10 11 — 10 9 8 7 6 5 4 3 2

A catalog record for this book is available from the Library of Congress.

0-664-22581-0

For those who first inspired me to study Scripture—
my grandmother, Flossie Bates; my mother, Mary Elmina Laha; and
the one who inspires me still, my wife, Sally Ann Laha

Contents

Series Introduction

The Bible has long been revered for its witness to God's presence and redeeming activity in the world; its message of creation and judgment, love and forgiveness, grace and hope; its memorable characters and stories; its challenges to human life; and its power to shape faith. For generations people have found in the Bible inspiration and instruction, and, for nearly as long, commentators and scholars have assisted students of the Bible. This series, Interpretation Bible Studies (IBS), continues that great heritage of scholarship with a fresh approach to biblical study.

Designed for ease and flexibility of use for either personal or group study, IBS helps readers not only to learn about the history and theology of the Bible, understand the sometimes difficult language of biblical passages, and marvel at the biblical accounts of God's activity in human life, but also to accept the challenge of the Bible's call to discipleship. IBS offers sound guidance for deepening one's knowledge of the Bible and for faithful Christian living in today's world.

IBS was developed out of three primary convictions. First, the Bible is the church's scripture and stands in a unique place of authority in Christian understanding. Second, good scholarship helps readers understand the truths of the Bible and sharpens their perception of God speaking through the Bible. Third, deep knowledge of the Bible bears fruit in one's ethical and spiritual life.

Each IBS volume has ten brief units of key passages from a book of the Bible. By moving through these units, readers capture the sweep of the whole biblical book. Each unit includes study helps, such as maps, photos, definitions of key terms, questions for reflection, and suggestions for resources for further study. In the back of each volume is a Leader's Guide that offers helpful suggestions on how to use IBS.

The Interpretation Bible Studies series grows out of the well-known Interpretation commentaries (John Knox Press), a series that helps preachers and teachers in their preparation. Although each IBS volume bears a deep kinship to its companion Interpretation commentary, IBS can stand alone. The reader need not be familiar with the Interpretation commentary to benefit from IBS. However, those who want to discover even more about the Bible will benefit by consulting Interpretation commentaries too.

Through the kind of encounter with the Bible encouraged by the Interpretation Bible Studies, the church will continue to discover God speaking afresh in the scriptures.

Introduction to Jeremiah

The book of Jeremiah is difficult to understand. It is a long and complex mixture of poetry and prose that, historically speaking, seems to follow no particular order. It is both a dismal and hopeful work, displaying a creative imagination almost unparalleled in the whole of scripture. It juxtaposes images of death with images of hope, giving us a variety of voices to translate as we seek to understand its meaning in history and in our present time. As R. P. Carroll notes so well in his book *Jeremiah*, "The reader who is not confused by reading the book of Jeremiah has not understood it" (9).

Like the casual reader, the scholarly community is equally confused by this unique book, as evidenced by the varied works appearing over the past fifteen to twenty years. At present, there seems to be very little agreement among this community about the origins and meanings of this book. The debate among scholars is compounded by the long oral traditions of prophecy and the later written traditions of prophecy expanded upon by numerous editors in an attempt to explain and interpret these prophecies, a process covering at least two hundred fifty years. One example of this later expansion is evidenced in the existence of two different versions of Jeremiah, one written in Greek (the Septuagint) and the other written in Hebrew (the Masoretic Text). These two versions vary in length and order and point to the difficulty of determining what, if any, portions of the book might be products of that particular time and place in history which led to the dismantling of the northern and southern kingdoms of Israel. Another example of this expansion is evidenced in Deuteronomistic portions of the book, that is, those portions

> "Predominantly, however, Jeremiah's book contains a message of hope. This message of hope, set against the background of political disaster and immense human suffering that accompanied it, gives the book its essential character." R. E. Clements, *Jeremiah*, Interpretation, 3.

which display a similarity of style, language, and thought to the material found in Joshua, Judges, 1 and 2 Samuel and 1 and 2 Kings. This Deuteronomistic influence is seen mostly in sermons and stories where the prophet appears to reflect on the present circumstances from the theological vantage point expressed in those earlier works. This long and complicated history behind the formation of the book leaves us to struggle with what John Bright calls "a hopeless hodge-podge thrown together without any discernable principle of arrangement at all" (lvi).

Scholars also disagree about the man Jeremiah. Some, like Carroll, suggest that we should "treat the character of Jeremiah as a work of fiction and recognize the impossibility of moving from the book to the real 'historical' Jeremiah" (12). Others, such as Bright and Henry McKeating, suggest that Jeremiah is a real person who lived and worked in a particular place and time, a person who can be known, at least in part, and who is one of the most important thinkers in the Old Testament. In either case, the words attributed to the prophet in this book helped Israel make sense of the tragic things it was experiencing and at the same time, helped it find some measure of hope for the future.

> "No braver or more tragic figure ever trod the stage of Israel's history than the prophet Jeremiah. His was the authentic voice of Mosaic Yahwism speaking, as it were, out of season to the dying nation. It was his lot through a long lifetime to say, and say again, that Judah was doomed and that that doom was Yahweh's righteous judgment upon her for her breach of covenant." John Bright, *A History of Israel*, 4th ed., 333.

As the book unfolds, the prophet Jeremiah, real or imagined, participates in the life and death of a people. He serves God not only in his words but, just as importantly, in his deeds. Like others in Judah, he suffers the pain and failure of a life in exile. Some scholars see him and his message as Christlike, that is, one whose person and message is acquainted with grief but also is aware of a new future awaiting us in God's love.

While current scholarship seems to be at an impasse concerning the precise history and meaning of the book of Jeremiah, this ancient work still serves to help "men and women overtaken by tragedies to face them, to respond courageously to them, and to look in hope beyond them. Although many of the prophecies necessarily look back upon events belonging to an irreversible past, they do so in a manner designed to promote a deep and certain hope in the future" (Clements, 3).

This short study is designed to give the reader a taste of the rich theological food offered in the book of Jeremiah. It offers a sampler platter of the major themes of the book with the hope that in tasting something of the ideas, attitudes, and experiences of this formative period in Israel's history, we might better savor those things that can nourish our lives in this present time.

Realizing the limitations of such a short study, the reader is encouraged to spend time reading and contemplating the full text of Jeremiah as it now appears in our Bibles. Reading and studying the text itself, without the aid of this or any other study, can be a rewarding experience. I would therefore conclude this introduction with a quote from *Italo Calvino* as offered by R. P. Carroll in *Jeremiah*:

The reading of a classic ought to give us a surprise or two vis-a-vis the notion that we had of it. For this reason, I can never sufficiently highly recommend the direct reading of the text itself, leaving aside the critical biography, commentaries, and interpretations as much as possible. Schools and universities ought to help us understand that no book that talks about a book says more than the book in question, but instead they do their level best to make us think the opposite. There is a widespread topsy-turviness of values whereby the introduction, critical apparatus, and bibliography are used as a smokescreen to hide what the text has to say and, indeed, can say only if left to speak for itself without intermediaries who claim to know more than the text does. (14)

Want to Know More?

About leading Bible study groups? See Roberta Hestenes, *Using the Bible in Groups* (Philadelphia: Westminster Press, 1983); Christine Blair, *The Art of Teaching the Bible* (Louisvill, Ky.: Geneva Press, 2001).

About the content or themes of Jeremiah? See R. E. Clements, *Jeremiah*, Interpretation: A Bible Commentary for Teaching and Preaching (Louisville, Ky.: John Knox Press, 1988), 1–12; R. E. Clements, *Old Testament Prophecy: From Oracles to Canon* (Louisville, Ky.: Westminster John Knox Press, 1996), 107–41.

About the prophet Jeremiah? See John M. Bracke, *Jeremiah 1–29*, Westminster Bible Companion (Louisville, Ky.: Westminster John Knox Press, 2000), 1–3; John Bright, *A History of Israel*, 4th ed. (Louisville, Ky.: Westminster John Knox Press, 2000), 333–36.

About the prophets of the fall of Judah and the exile? See Celia Brewer Marshall, *A Guide through the Old Testament* (Louisville, Ky.: Westminster John Knox Press, 1989), 108–21.

Jeremiah's World

The book of Jeremiah concerns itself with the events surrounding the downfall of Judah and culminating with the destruction of Jerusalem and its temple in 587 B.C.E. In his book *To Pluck Up, To Tear Down*, Walter Brueggemann claims that "this crisis is the dominant and shaping event of the entire Old Testament" (1). Certainly, the downfall of Judah seems to jeopardize Yahweh's covenant promise of land and progeny to his chosen people. It seems that the unique relationship between God and his people may have come to an end.

A new, powerful threat has emerged on the scene: Babylon. This menacing power had already captured the northern kingdom of Israel and was now in a position to take over the southern kingdom of Judah, the last remnant of the once great Jewish nation. A compounding threat lay to the south of Judah: its old nemesis Egypt. What we discover in the book of Jeremiah is a succession of kings, all sons of the great reformer Josiah, who foolishly try to placate first one of these great powers and then the other. Then, after finally provoking the stronger of the two, Babylon, to invade its territories and assume governance of its capital city, Jerusalem, most of the citizens of Judah are sent packing to the hinterlands of Babylon.

While historians might view these developments simply from the standpoint of competing political and military entities, Jeremiah views them from the standpoint of a mistaken theology. According to Jeremiah, Israel and Judah have failed to keep covenant with God.

> Israel normally refers to the ten northern tribes, though theologically it can also be used for the entire nation of both the northern and southern kingdoms. F. L. Cross, ed., *The Oxford Dictionary of the Christian Church* (Oxford: Oxford University Press, 1958, 1974).

They have ignored their God-given responsibilities to do justice and instead do whatever it pleases them to do, all the while counting on Yahweh to protect them should they get into trouble. Of course, they do get into trouble—with God—and it falls to Jeremiah to point out the error of their ways. Jeremiah announces Yahweh's judgment to the people in general, and to the various rulers of the court and temple more specifically. Jeremiah's announcements of judgment fall on deaf ears, in part because of the commonly held belief that Yahweh had made certain irrevocable promises to the monarchy, to the temple, and to Judah guaranteeing their safety and security. Jeremiah challenges this belief and calls over and over again for Judah to repent and to return to Yahweh and to covenant keeping as the only possible means of avoiding a repeat of history, a history of exile, death, and destruction.

The Kings of Judah

The kings of Judah as listed in Jeremiah (all dates B.C.E.)

Josiah, 640–609
Jehoahaz II, 609
Jehoiakim, 609–598
Jehoiachin, 598–97
Zedekiah, 597–587
Gedaliah, 587–582

Chapters 36 through 39 provide us with the setting for Jeremiah's work. They show us the problems confronting Judah, and Jeremiah's role in identifying and explaining these problems. They are also pivotal for understanding how the prophecies of Jeremiah were written down and understood as the word of God. And they show us how the word of God functions in both the downfall of Judah and in her life during exile.

The Making of a Scroll

Among other things, chapter 36 provides us with a behind-the-scenes look at Bible making. Here we see something unique in all of scripture, namely, the story of how Yahweh's word comes to Jeremiah with the instructions to have all that Yahweh says recorded on a scroll so that "it may be that when the house of Judah hears of all the disasters that I intend to do to them, all of them may turn from their evil ways, so that I may forgive their iniquity and their sin" (v. 3). Here we see the beginning of the transition from oral to written prophecy. This written word, this "Bible" if you will, emerges in the midst of a major social upheaval, and it does so with the expressed purpose of moving Judah to repentance. In other words, this written word, like the oral renderings of the word before it, is designed to transform and renew life. It is intended to be read and heard in and among the people of God so that, together, they might find their way back into God's favor and thus be spared the pain of exile.

Following God's instructions, Jeremiah enlists the aid of a scribe named Baruch to write down the prophecies God gives to him. He then instructs Baruch to go to the temple, from which Jeremiah has been barred from entering, and to read the word of God to the assembled people. Baruch dutifully follows Jeremiah's instructions. Apparently, some of the gathered officials were so taken with this word from the Lord that they took it upon themselves to share it with the king. The scene quickly shifts to the king, who is cold and calculating in his contempt for this word from the Lord. Sitting in front of his fireplace, the king begins cutting the scroll into small pieces with his knife, and then he throws the pieces into the fire. After engaging in this early form of "document shredding", the king then issues an arrest warrant for both Jeremiah and Baruch. "But the Lord hid them" (v. 26b). With this brief notation, we are given notice that more is going on here than meets the eye.

There is great irony in what happens next. God commands a second scroll to be made following the same process as the first one. Only this time, "many similar words were added to them" (v. 32b). By refusing to listen to the word of God, "the king eventually brings about a situation in which a far greater number, both of his and of succeeding generations, become hearers of this word" (Clements, 214). So instead of destroying the word of God, the king's calculated actions give rise to even more words from God.

> "By refusing to hear this prophetic word, the king eventually brought about a situation in which a far greater number, both of his and of succeeding generations, became hearers of this word. . . . Far from destroying the word of God, Jehoiakim's attempt to burn the scroll of Jeremiah's prophecies led only to its acquiring new force and range." R. E. Clements, *Jeremiah*, Interpretation, 214.

The transition from oral to written prophecy prompts a whole new perspective on the mind and will of God. It gives rise to a wide-ranging body of literature that provides, first to Judaism and later to the church, new insights into the nature and being of God. But, as Brueggemann maintains, "scroll-making is a daring, dangerous enterprise. . . . [I]t is paradigmatic of the way in which God counters human pretension and resistence. God will not leave the king scroll-less, even if the king wants no scroll" (*To Build, To Plant,* 137–38). Because it was, and is, God's word, and because as Isaiah says, "the word of our God will stand forever" (Isa. 40:8), it is reproduced and added to so that more and more people, along with the king, can come to know what God desires from them.

Prophet and King

Judah's life as an independent nation is fast drawing to a close. Jeremiah continues to deliver God's warning to the court and temple establishment: Repent and live, or resist and die. Under the leadership of Zedekiah, Judah remains stubbornly steadfast in its resistance to God's word, a mistake that leads toward the nation's death.

Judah is increasingly caught between the warring superpowers of her age: Egypt to the southwest and Babylon to the north and west. Zedekiah and his capital city of Jerusalem are increasingly put at risk by these political and military powers, but, as Jeremiah tries to make clear, these are not the only powers about which to worry. Jeremiah continues to argue that Judah is, in large measure, responsible for the mess it is in because of its failure to honor the ways of Yahweh. In fact, he argues that these threatening powers are instruments of God's judgment. So we find the prophet demanding that Judah find new ways of honoring its God even in the midst of its growing oppression from these two competing superpowers.

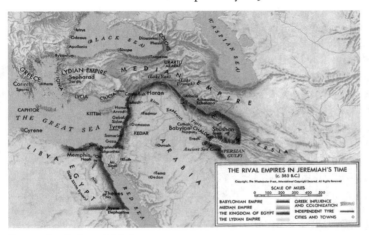

The empires in Jeremiah's time

With the opening verses of chapter 37, we learn that Jerusalem is under siege from the Babylonians. To our surprise, Zedekiah asks for Jeremiah to pray for the city (v. 3). While we do not know if Jeremiah honored the king's request, we do know that the siege was temporarily lifted because of a perceived threat from Egypt. This is an act that causes some in Jerusalem to think that all the harsh prophecies of Jeremiah have been fulfilled and that things will begin to turn around in their favor. However, Jeremiah delivers another message from Yahweh telling the king and his constituents that they are not to be deceived by these new developments because Yahweh's judgment against Judah is not yet complete. In fact, the prophet announces that the Babylonians will return, and when they do, they will sack and burn the city (v. 8). Once again, the Jerusalem establishment not only misreads Babylon, it misreads Yahweh.

> "[Zedekiah] is a man trapped between the Babylonians and his own princes: he cannot resolve his problems because whichever way he turns he faces disaster." R. P. Carroll, *Jeremiah*, Old Testament Library (Philadelphia: Westminster Press, 1986), 686.

During this brief lifting of the siege, Jeremiah leaves the city for awhile to tend to some personal business. Upon his return he is charged with desertion, beaten, and thrown into prison (vv. 13–16).

Once again, Zedekiah sends for Jeremiah. This time he secretly questions the prophet about whether or not he has any new word from the Lord. Apparently, the king believes that Jeremiah possesses unique information, information he desperately needs but cannot seem to get from his advisors. True to form, Jeremiah answers, "There is! You will be handed over to the king of Babylon" (v. 17). The king's response to this familiar and unwelcome message is not recorded. What is recorded is Jeremiah's pleading with the king for more favorable treatment, trying, perhaps, to draw a distinction between the message and the messenger. For some unknown reason, the king grants the prophet's request and confines him to the less restrictive "court of the guard" instead of returning him to prison.

With the opening verses of chapter 38, we find the princely rulers beginning to exercise power in their own right. They see their world crumbling before their very eyes and they see Jeremiah and his frightful words as another unwelcome threat to their powers and policies. Understandably, they seek to rid themselves of this menace by petitioning the king to have him put to death. In a scene remarkably like the one of Jesus before Pilate (John 19:6), we see Zedekiah abdicating his power and delivering Jeremiah into the hands of these other authorities who straightforwardly proceed to throw him into a muddy cistern.

Jeremiah is rescued once more, this time by a foreign court official who petitions the king for Jeremiah's release. And once more, we are given notice that more is going on here than meets the eye (cf. 36:26).

The scene then changes back to more familiar territory, a series of point-counterpoint exchanges between Jeremiah and Zedekiah. Surprisingly, these exchanges are not hostile in nature but show genuine efforts from both prophet and king to truly communicate with one another. Once again, the king needs information that his advisors apparently do not have. Here we see with Brueggemann that "the book of Jeremiah is insistent in its claim that the prophet carries the data the king needs, which the king cannot receive from any other source" (*To Build, To Plant*, 151). A strange alliance develops between Jeremiah and Zedekiah. The prophet and king lean on each other. The king leans on the prophet for needed information, and the prophet leans on the king for personal protection. But this new alliance in no way alters Jeremiah's message. God's judgment is fast approaching, and it now appears that there is nothing Jeremiah or Zedekiah can do to stop it.

> "Jeremiah offered King Zedekiah an option to spare his life and also to spare Jerusalem from being burned by surrendering to the Babylonians (38:17). Zedekiah wavered, waited too long, and finally, as Jeremiah warned, was 'not able to escape from their hand' (38:18). In Zedekiah's punishment, God's word is fulfilled." John M. Bracke, *Jeremiah 30–52 and Lamentations*, Westminster Bible Companion (Louisville, Ky.: Westminster John Knox Press, 1999), 76–77.

The Downfall of Jerusalem

As we will continue to see in subsequent chapters, Jeremiah's words to Judah and its various leaders are consistent from beginning to end: Judah can repent of its considerable sins and turn again to God, an act that will lead to a prolonged life, or Judah can continue resisting God, an act that will inevitably lead to its downfall and destruction. Time is of the essence, for soon the chance to repent and turn back the tidal wave of destruction will be past.

In chapter 39, Judah continues in its resistence to God, and finally has to pay the price: "In the ninth year of King Zedekiah of Judah, in the tenth month, King Nebuchadrezzar of Babylon and all his army came against Jerusalem and besieged it; in the eleventh year of Zedekiah, in the fourth month, on the ninth day of the month, a breach was made in the city. . . . Jerusalem was taken" (vv. 1–3; see also Jer. 52:4–16 and 2 Kgs. 25:1–12).

Jeremiah spends his entire career trying to get the various kings of Judah to understand the high costs of resisting God, but his words fall on deaf ears. Finally, the die is cast and the threat of Babylon becomes real. Toward the end of its life as an independent nation, the only helpful thing left for Judah to do is to accept its punishment by surrendering to the Babylonians and facing the consequences of a life of sin. But Judah resists such a move with all its might, foolishly believing it can somehow still find a way to prevail over its enemies and continue on with the life it had chosen for itself. This resistance proves to be a bad mistake.

Judgment finally arrives, and Judah now discovers that its mistaken theology has led not only to religious consequences but also to political, military, and economic consequences.

With the fall of Jerusalem, Zedekiah quietly steals away under the cover of darkness, leaving his people to fend for themselves. The conquering army gives chase and overtakes him on the plains of Jericho (v. 5). What happens next is both swift and brutal. Zedekiah is taken to King Nebuchadrezzar, who makes him watch the systematic slaughtering of first his sons and then his noblemen. Then Zedekiah's own eyes are put out, and he is bound in chains and shipped to the outskirts of Babylon. The narrative resumes with the "tearing down" of Jerusalem and the "plucking up of her people" for a life in exile. Ironically, only the poor are left in and around Jerusalem, the very ones neglected and abused by the religious and political authorities of old Judah. In a twist of fate, they are given "vineyards and fields" (v. 10) under the new authority of the king of Babylon.

Chapter 39 moves to conclusion with a brief but important story about the prophet Jeremiah. The king of Babylon orders that Jeremiah be attended to and given safe lodging in the place where he had once enjoyed Zedekiah's protection, that is, in the "court of the guard" (vv. 14–15; see also 38:28).

It can be assumed that Nebuchadrezzar knows something about Jeremiah and his prophecies, perhaps even the story of Jeremiah urging Zedekiah to surrender. How ironic then that Jeremiah, the one accused as being a traitor to Judah by looking favorably on Babylon, is here granted protection by Babylon. Even though this act could be construed as some sort of vindication for the charges leveled against Jeremiah by Jewish authorities, there is a more important message. What this act proves is that Jeremiah's prophecies and admonitions were on target. As Brueggemann puts it, "[Jeremiah] had urged 'submit and live.' As one who submitted, he is permitted to live" (*To Build, To Plant*, 158).

While much of the emphasis here, and throughout the entire book of Jeremiah, is on the sweeping destruction of Jerusalem and the house of David, there is nevertheless an element of hope. Not only are Jeremiah and a few of Jerusalem's poor spared from the death and destruction, but so too is Ebed-melech, a man many scholars view as an important and symbolic remnant of the faith community. From this perspective, the message is clear. Those who go their own way, cling to their own powers, and turn deaf ears to God meet with destruction and death. In contrast, those who go God's way, cling to God's powers, and give attention to God's word, meet with new possibilities for life. This is, perhaps, one of the most basic messages in all of scripture.

> "For I will surely save you, and you shall not fall by the sword; but you shall have your life as a prize of war, because you have trusted in me, says the LORD." Jeremiah 39:18.

Chapters 36–39 provide us with a historical overview of the entire book of Jeremiah. They reveal the twin themes of Judah's sin and rebellion and Yahweh's announcement of judgment given through the spoken and written word of the prophet. They reveal the horrible consequences of sin as seen in the utter destruction of Judah and its once proud and glorious capital city, Jerusalem. But they also reveal a glimmer of hope, a hope for life after exile. It falls to us to keep this glimmer of hope alive as we study the distinctive perspective that Jeremiah offers us concerning the God who "plucks up and pulls down, who destroys and overthrows, who builds and plants" (1:10).

 ## Want to Know More?

About the Babylonian Empire? See Paul J. Achtemeier, ed., *HarperCollins Bible Dictionary*, rev. ed. (New York: HarperCollins, 1996), 97–99.

About Baruch? See *HarperCollins Bible Dictionary*, 105–6.

About Judah? See *HarperCollins Bible Dictionary*, 550–51.

About the prophets in the last days of Judah? See John Bright, *A History of Israel*, 4th ed. (Louisville, Ky.: Westminster John Knox Press, 2000), 331–40.

? Questions for Reflection

1. What role does repentance play in Jeremiah's theology? What are the similarities and/or differences in your theology?
2. Compare and contrast Zedekiah's abdication of responsibility in Jeremiah 38 to that of Pilate in John 19. In what sense do we "wash our hands" of responsibility in our churches, our homes, our workplaces, and our communities?
3. How does God use the prophets to speak to the kings? What are the implications for the church's role in speaking to modern governing authorities?
4. How do you understand the relationship between sin and judgment? How is your understanding similar to or different from that of Jeremiah?

The Call of Jeremiah

Chapter 1 is a microcosm of the first half of the book of Jeremiah. It includes the proclamation of God's word by his chosen prophet, the idea of God's sovereignty over Judah and all the nations around it, the rejection of God's word and its tragic consequences, and the hint of hope lodged with God to create life out of death.

It is generally agreed that the opening verses are the work of editors. Even so, this introductory segment (vv. 1–3) "provides information, whatever its historical reliability may be, without which it would be difficult to understand the book" (Carroll, *Jeremiah*, 25). It locates Jeremiah and his prophetic work in and around the time of Josiah, king of Judah, and his sons, Jehoiakim and Zedekiah, Josiah's immediate successors, which gives us a time frame somewhere around 627 B.C.E. to the fall of Jerusalem in 587 B.C.E. It also tells us some things about Jeremiah the man: He was part of the priestly clan of Anathoth, and he was a man chosen by Yahweh to convey his message to the people of Judah. Thus, Jeremiah is identified as a fully authorized spokesperson for Yahweh so that there is to be no distinction between Jeremiah's words and Yahweh's words.

> "Before I formed you in the womb I knew you, and before you were born I consecrated you; I appointed you a prophet to the nations." Jeremiah 1:4–5.

The notation of these specific kings of Judah and the notation that "the word of the Lord" came during these specific times signals that there is more than one governing reality to be dealt with in Judah. "The word of the Lord" comes to and through real people, in real times and circumstances, to claim its rightful place in the affairs of men and women. And, as we shall see, it is a word that will not go away.

The final words of this editorial preface, "until the captivity of Jerusalem" (v. 3b), provide us with a glimpse of where this book is headed. They clue us in on God's intention to dismantle Judah and to drive his people into exile. It is a powerful and terrifying word that will not cease until it accomplishes its purpose.

The Providence of God

"The word of the Lord came to me" (v. 4) is a phrase we will see over and over again throughout the book of Jeremiah. It serves as an indicator that what follows is not something dreamed up by the prophet, but something that Yahweh had commanded him to speak. It indicates an overwhelming experience with God's revelation that shapes everything Jeremiah says and does.

And how and when does such revelation come to Jeremiah? In the first place, it comes to him in an extraordinary way: "Before I formed you in the womb I knew you, before you were born, I consecrated you" (v. 5). This sweeping affirmation speaks to the providence and sovereignty of God who involves himself in the everyday affairs of the world. It makes it clear that Jeremiah's birth and his vocation are coterminous, meaning that there was never a time in which Jeremiah was not summoned as God's spokesperson.

"No one could confirm or deny that he [Jeremiah] possessed this calling; it was between himself and God. . . . It was a supremely private event to Jeremiah, while at the same time public, national, and ultimately international in its significance and consequences." R. E. Clements, *Jeremiah,* Interpretation, 16.

According to William Holladay, the three verbs—"formed," "knew," and "consecrated" (v. 5)—are to be understood together, as they all speak to a deeply intimate relationship and to covenantal obligation (Holladay, *Jeremiah 1*, 33–34). Again, the point is that Jeremiah is God's spokesperson, which is to say that Jeremiah belongs to God and speaks for God, a point made clear in the remainder of verse 5: "I appointed you a prophet to the nations." This is indeed the stuff of providence.

God elects, calls, commissions, and empowers individuals and nations to do God's work. This is the experience of Jeremiah, and it is an experience that is repeated in the lives of other believers in every time and place.

Human Protest

Whenever we experience the word of the Lord, it is perhaps our nature to shrink in the face of such awesome power. Jeremiah's initial reaction to this word is less than enthusiastic. In words reminiscent of Moses (cf. Exod. 4:10), Jeremiah says he doesn't know how to speak, offering the excuse that he is only a boy (v. 6). One wonders who would know how to speak "to the nations"? It is hard enough to speak God's word to an individual friend or family member. How would you like to be charged with the responsibility to speak God's word to priests, kings, and nations? It is no wonder then that Jeremiah protests such an overwhelming calling. It is a posture we will see again in his so-called confessions (see unit 6).

God's Word in Human Mouths

God's response to Jeremiah speaks again to the nature of providence and God's sovereign rule over individuals and nations. Jeremiah's excuses are irrelevant in light of God's intentions. God will have his way with Jeremiah and with the nations to whom God will speak through the prophet. So, God thunders, "Do not say, 'I am only a boy'; for you shall go to all to whom I send you, and you shall speak whatever I command you. Do not be afraid of them, for I am with you to deliver you" (vv. 7–8).

This strong response from God moves the emphasis from the personal struggles of a man and back onto the sovereign word of God, which is everywhere active and powerful, creating and re-creating at will, aligning the course of history in conformity to God's will. It is a word that will have its way with the prophet, the king, and the nations. It is a word that is both terrifying and comforting precisely because it is God's word. It is terrifying because of the awesome responsibilities it

Key Terms

Covenant relationship A relationship between God and persons or groups of persons marked either by God's unilateral promises or by mutual agreements, and marked especially by human promises for obedience to God's will.

Election God's choosing of a people to enjoy the benefits of salvation and to carry out God's purposes in the world.

Call God's summons to salvation or to a particular work of service, implying a divine selection.

From Donald K. McKim, *Westminster Dictionary of Theological Terms* (Louisville, Ky.: Westminster John Knox Press, 1996).

brings; it is comforting because it is accompanied by God's presence and power.

It is worth noting here that the admonition, "Do not be afraid . . . , for I am with you," is a familiar, almost archetypal theme in scripture. Fear is commonly felt and expressed in Scripture. It is felt most intensely in times of confrontation with God and God's work. Sometimes it is a fear of the unknown, or a fear of having to face God, or a fear of not being able to do what one feels God is calling one to do. For example, Abraham is afraid when he feels he cannot measure up to God's expectations (e.g., Gen. 15:1; 26:24; 46:3), Moses is afraid when he encounters God on the mountain (Exod. 3:6), Samuel is afraid when he realizes the nature of his call (1 Sam. 3:15), the nation of Israel is afraid when, because of its calling, it has to deal with hostile forces (e.g., Isa. 41:10; 43:5), Mary is afraid when she is confronted by an angel (Luke 1:30), and Paul is afraid when he takes God's word to Corinth (1 Cor. 2:3). These and many other examples of being fearful in light of the awesome nature of God's work are all met with the same response: "I am with you." It is a reassuring and comforting response; it is a response that moves us toward incarnation, reminding us that God is indeed God-with-us.

In the providence of God, Jeremiah is called forth to a new and important work. It is a work he feels ill-equipped to perform, and so he protests. But God overrides his protest and reminds him that he is not being asked to perform this work on his own. And then, in an effort to make these words of reassurance become real for him, God performs a sign: "Then the LORD put out his hand and touched my mouth; and the LORD said to me: 'Now I have put my words in your mouth'" (v. 9).

Here again God's word and God's actions are intertwined. Yahweh speaks to Jeremiah and then reaches out to touch his mouth (cf. Isa. 6:6–7). Here the prophet is readied to proclaim God's word. Yahweh takes the initiative by putting his words into Jeremiah's mouth so that Jeremiah's words are to be heard and understood as Yahweh's words (see also 5:14; 15:16, 19).

> The phrase "Do not be afraid, for I am with you" is a familiar one in Scripture. Read the following passages where one of God's people was afraid: Gen. 15:1; Exod. 3:6; 1 Sam. 3:15; Isa. 41:10; Luke 1:30; 1 Cor. 2:3.

This sign is the last component in a well-established pattern in the Old Testament for calling and commissioning. We see this pattern, for instance, in the calling and commissioning of both Moses and Gideon. There are four basic components: the call or commissioning, an objection from the one being called, some offer of reassurance from the one who calls, and some sort of sign to legitimate the calling. In the case of Jeremiah, Moses, and Gideon, these four basic components may be outlined as follows (see Holladay, *Jeremiah 1*, 27–28):

Call	Jer. 1:5	Exod. 3:10	Judg. 6:14
Objection	Jer. 1:6	Exod. 3:11	Judg. 6:15
Reassurance	Jer. 1:7–8	Exod. 3:12	Judg. 6:16
Sign	Jer. 1:9	Exod. 3:12	Judg. 6:17–22

Pulling Down and Building Up

After calling Jeremiah to the position of prophet, and after reassuring Jeremiah that he would be with him, and after touching Jeremiah's mouth to infuse it with his own words, God finally lets Jeremiah, and us, in on what he proposes to tell the nations: "See, today I appoint you over nations and over kingdoms, to pluck up and to pull down, to destroy and to overthrow, to build and to plant" (v. 10).

Contrary to most people's understanding of "call" today, Jeremiah's calling involves him in the political affairs of his day. God sets him over and against nations and kingdoms. This understanding is basic to the work of all the Old Testament prophets, for more often than not, their calling is to speak to matters of national and international importance. As the book of Jeremiah makes clear, Yahweh is not just the God of Judah but is the God of the whole world. In ancient Israel, religion and politics are united; there is no separation of church and state. The work of Jeremiah the prophet therefore affects the whole of ordered life, religious and political. Indeed, his work involves nothing less than the rebuilding of the world.

Before God can rebuild the world, however, he must first tear down the old one. This is the bold and unpopular announcement Jeremiah is called upon to make. The full scope of God's impending work is caught up in these pregnant and provocative words: "pluck up" and "pull down," "destroy" and "overthrow," "build" and "plant" (v. 10). Re-creation and renewal requires the tearing down and dismantling of old and useless structures. This, of course, is a difficult and often unwelcome work because it means letting go of old hopes and dreams and trying to imagine something new that, as of yet, does not exist. It is no wonder, then, that this new work Jeremiah announces is met with strong opposition. These pregnant and provocative words also assert that there is no structure or policy of church or state that can overturn God's judgment or close off God's new work. God alone has the power to alter the course of history by bringing to a close those things that oppose his will and creating anew those things that might better serve his purposes (cf. Deut. 32:39; Isa. 45:7).

Walter Brueggemann suggests that the six verbs in verse 10 provide us with "the essential shape of the book of Jeremiah in its present form" (*To Pluck Up*, 24). He persuasively argues that the main focus of the book of Jeremiah is on the dismantling of Judah and its beloved capital city, Jerusalem, along with a hopeful nod to the future rebuilding of that city, with both the dismantling and the rebuilding being ordered and directed by Yahweh. Brueggemann also argues that this same notion of endings and beginnings is picked up in John 2:19 and cleverly used by Jesus to interpret God's new saving work to be wrought in crucifixion and resurrection: "In those early claims for Jesus, the early Church derives its understanding of the historical process from prophetic faith, and perhaps precisely from Jeremiah. In both cases, Jeremiah and Jesus, the text invites one to reckon with the reality of discontinuity in the historical process out of which God can work a powerful newness, utterly inexplicable" (*To Pluck Up*, 25).

It falls to Jeremiah to articulate these bold claims to people who do not want to hear such words. The leaders of court and temple continue to rule with the mistaken notion that God will protect Judah from all harm. Nothing could be further from the truth. God will not protect them. Instead, God will order the dismantling of their neat little world as judgment for their sins. This is the burdensome word Jeremiah is commissioned to share with his people.

Visions of Things to Come

After being called and commissioned, and after being told about the burdensome nature of his work, Jeremiah is given two visions that bring clarity to Yahweh's initiatives. The first of these visions involves an almond tree and an interesting play on words. God asks Jeremiah what he sees and he responds by saying he sees—*shaqed* in Hebrew— an almond branch. Then God says, "You have seen well, for I am watching [*shoqed* in Hebrew] over my word to perform it" (v. 12). The focus here is on God's watching—watching over the words he gives to Jeremiah to speak. The intended point is to assure Jeremiah that, while people may not immediately understand that Jeremiah's words are indeed God's words, God will watch over his own words to assure that they accomplish his purpose. God's watching speaks to that which is beyond human management or control. Another power is at work in the world besides the power exercised in temple and court. Yahweh manages and controls all other powers, even those of Babylon, making all powers but his own provisional at best.

In the second vision, Jeremiah sees a boiling pot lying on its side, pointing away from the north (v. 13). God then proceeds to tell Jeremiah what this vision is meant to convey. It shows the coming of an unnamed power from the north that will set itself over and against all the cities of Judah as God's judgment upon them because of their many sins (vv. 14–16). God is telling Jeremiah that the "plucking up and pulling down" he is called to announce will be brought about by a superior political and military force. Judah will have to contend with a new adversary on the world's stage, one that, like itself, is controlled by Almighty God, and one that will eventually bring Judah to ruin. Here again we see the absolute sovereignty of God, who alone has the power to cause nations to come and go according to God's own purpose. Taken together, these two visions point to the dominant theme of the entire book of Jeremiah: the forceful dismantling of Judah's religious and political life as fair judgment for her continued sin and

"And I said, 'I see a branch of an almond tree.'"

"Jeremiah 1 begins with an affirmation that the word of the Lord will bring about the captivity of Jerusalem. Jeremiah 1 concludes with a warning that the word of the Lord, spoken by God's messenger, Jeremiah, will be resisted by the Jerusalem religious and political establishment, who have forsaken God." John M. Bracke, *Jeremiah 1–29*, Westminster Bible Companion (Louisville, Ky.: Westminster John Knox Press, 1999), 22.

rebellion. This is the theme that will require Jeremiah to gird up his loins, stand tall, and give voice to Yahweh's commands, else he succumb to the same fate as Judah (v. 17).

A Little Encouragement

For all the impending chaos about to be loosed on the world, chapter 1 ends as it begins—with a personal word to Jeremiah. The God who formed, knew, and consecrated Jeremiah before he was born, the God who told Jeremiah not to be afraid, now, in light of the burdensome word Jeremiah must declare to the nations, reaffirms his providential care.

 Want to Know More?

About the call of the prophets? See Horst Dietrich Preuss, *Old Testament Theology*, vol. 2 (Louisville, Ky.: Westminster John Knox Press, 1996), 67–69; Brevard S. Childs, *Isaiah*, Old Testament Library (Louisville, Ky.: Westminster John Knox Press, 2000), 52–53.

About covenant? See Donald K. McKim, *Westminster Dictionary of Theological Terms* (Louisville, Ky: Westminster John Knox Press, 1996), 64; Gordon S. Wakefield, *The Westminster Dictionary of Christian Spirituality* (Philadelphia: Westminster Press, 1983), 98–99; Werner H. Schmidt, *Faith of the Old Testament: A History* (Philadelphia: Westminster Press, 1983), 106–9.

About election? See Horst Dietrich Preuss, *Old Testament Theology*, vol. 1 (Louisville, Ky.: Westminster John Knox Press, 1995), chap. 2.

God tells Jeremiah that he will be made "a fortified city, an iron pillar, and a bronze wall" to all those who will fight against him so that they shall not prevail against him (v. 18). And then God reiterates perhaps the most treasured words found in all of scripture: "I am with you . . .to deliver you" (v. 19).

These words are reminders that, ultimately, God's love will win over God's judgment, a claim Christians see validated in resurrection. Perhaps here these words offer another hint of a faithful remnant. If exceptions can be made to the deathly judgment against Judah and Jerusalem, perhaps there is a way for the exiled survivors to nurture hope. If God is indeed the one who "plucks up" and "pulls down," then God will have to be the one who also "builds" and "plants."

Questions for Reflection

1. How does one discern "the word of the Lord" today? How does one distinguish between God's word and other words?

2. What do we mean when we say God is sovereign over us and the world? In what ways can this be documented and affirmed?

3. Compare and contrast the call of Jeremiah in chapter 1 with the call of Moses in Exodus 4. How are people "called" today? How do we "protest" such calls?

4. Jeremiah suggests that Judah must "die" in order to "live," a teaching articulated and acted out by Jesus Christ. What might this mean for us?

3

Jeremiah 3:1-25

Unfaithfulness

In chapter 3, we find a familiar mix of poetry and prose that powerfully describes the unfaithfulness of Israel and Judah. Israel, of course, was long ago dismantled and dispersed. Given this history, one might expect Judah to have mended its ways in order to avoid a similar fate. Instead, Judah arrogantly congratulates itself on its escape and continues its life of unfaithfulness toward God as if it no longer cared about its relationship with God. The theme of unfaithfulness is developed using the metaphor of marriage introduced in chapter 2, with Yahweh as the husband and Judah as his bride. The language which follows is that of a lawsuit based on the marriage laws found in Deuteronomy 24, but with a twist. Here, Yahweh is both plaintiff and judge. Yahweh is portrayed as a faithful husband, providing for Judah in every conceivable way, and Judah is portrayed as an unfaithful wife, openly and defiantly chasing after other partners. Judah fails to realize that this "marriage" requires loyalty and trust and a lot of hard, disciplined work. To succeed, it cannot be an occasional affair.

As R. P. Carroll points out, some of the metaphors employed in this chapter are "quite obscene, but such obscenities are a feature of books such as Jeremiah and Ezekiel" (*Jeremiah*, 42). Judah is shown to be a whore, lying in wait to seduce one lover after another, all the while neglecting her rightful partner, Yahweh. Yahweh rightfully levels charges against her. According to the law codes of Deuteronomy, such circumstances precluded the husband from taking back an unfaithful wife because she would be considered defiled. Furthermore, attempts to reconcile under such circumstances would be considered attempts to defile the land, as sin was thought to have far-ranging consequences extending to every aspect of the created order.

In light of the accepted law of the times, it is absolutely amazing that Yahweh sends the prophet to persuade Judah to return to him and to resume a life of faithfulness with him. According to the law, Yahweh is expressly forbidden to take Judah back. Yet it appears that God's love is such that it can transcend the law. Against all expectations, Yahweh shows himself to be vulnerable in his great love for his people. Here we learn one of the fundamental lessons of scripture: God's ways are not our ways. God is free to do as God chooses to do, which, in fact, God seems to do on a regular basis, most often overriding law with love and grace. Our ways are something else altogether. Our ways are stubborn and foolish, often causing us to miss the experience of love and grace God is offering.

> "According to the law, Yahweh is expressly forbidden to take Judah back. Yet it appears that God's love is such that it can transcend the law."

Excursus

We should note before moving on that any metaphor can be misused and misunderstood. Metaphors certainly play a crucial role in helping us understand and interpret feelings, thoughts, constructs, relationships, and the like, but they have their limits. They can be pushed too far, causing the image to break down and lose its intended impact. This is especially true when metaphors employ anthropomorphic terms for God. Such terms are often the only way we have of conveying something about God in an understandable way, and yet it should also be obvious that an image of God as husband and/or father, for instance, can be fraught with problems. It is possible and even probable that such an image may be offensive or carry an unintended, or opposite, meaning to what it is intended to convey, as in the case of someone who might live in an abusive family. On the other hand, even when understood as intended, such a metaphor can never fully explain or exhaust the essence and being of God who, as theologians often say, is "wholly other." In any and all cases, the meaning

> "God language mirrors human relations, and it implicitly justifies human behavior. Much, but not all, of Jeremiah's God language justifies violence against women and subordinates them to their human kings, judges and fathers." Kathleen M. O'Connor, in *Women's Bible Commentary*, expanded ed., ed. Carol A. Newsom and Sharon H. Ringe, 180.

of a given metaphor changes according to its understanding and use in other times and places in history. Finally, with Simone Weil we know that when we try to speak of God there is nothing that resembles what we can conceive when we say that word. With this caveat, let us return to our text.

A Broken Marriage

Chapter 3 opens with a series of rhetorical questions: "If a man divorces his wife and she . . . becomes another man's wife, will he return to her? Would not such a land be greatly polluted? You have played the whore with many lovers; and would you return to me?" (v. 1). The answers are clear to anyone who knows the law codes. Judah's willful and consistent infidelities make reconciliation impossible.

Israel is encouraged to do some soul searching. Looking around, there seems to be no place where she has not broken covenant with God (v. 2). Like a prostitute working the streets, she waits for other lovers (cf. Hosea 3). God tries to get her attention by withholding the rains, an act that no doubt has an economic impact on her life. But Israel keeps on playing the role of a whore without any acknowledgment of shame (v. 3). God then points out that she still refers to him as father and friend, daring to ask God if he would stay angry even as she continues to flaunt her sin in front of him (vv. 4–5).

Key Terms

Anthropomorphic Describing the divine with human characteristics. The gods portrayed in Greco-Roman mythology are extremely anthropomorphic.

Repentance The act of expressing penitence and contrition for sin.

What we see here is the temptation to take God for granted, a temptation to which we still succumb. Like Israel, we live and act as if God is always available to us no matter how much we give ourselves to selfish and sinful behavior. Like Israel, we routinely use family language to address God as if he were our best buddy, ready at any time to come to our rescue.

Israel continues to talk the talk without attempting to walk the walk. She speaks of God "as if he was completely at her disposal when she should be at God's disposal" (Holladay, *Jeremiah 1*, 115). Israel seems to be hoping that God will somehow lose track of, or interest in, her wanton ways, but God sees everything she does. Her actions cause God's heart to ache with pain.

In verses 6–10, the focus narrows to Judah and its failure to learn from its kinsmen in the former northern kingdom. Judah watched as Israel sold itself in loose living. Judah saw the consequences its sister-state was forced to pay as judgment for its sins. Israel was issued a "decree of divorce" and was sent packing to a life in exile (v. 8). Yet Judah has learned nothing and has changed nothing. Judah gives a half-hearted nod to God when it suits her to do so, pretending that all is well with their relationship. But God knows the truth about their relationship and wants to repair it.

Attempt to Reconcile

What happens next is astounding. God sends Jeremiah to invite Israel back home, back into a covenant of "marriage" (v. 12). God is more than just a distraught lover lashing out in pain against his wayward partner; God is also one who longs for, and works for, some possibility of reunion. The invitation to return (*shub* in Hebrew) is one of the central doctrines in the book of Jeremiah (Clements, 35). What God wants more than anything else is for Israel to return to God with her whole heart. This, of course, requires an acknowledgment of guilt and genuine repentance on her part. According to most scholars, the invitation to return speaks to a desire that goes back to the time of Josiah, a desire for the reunion of the northern and southern kingdoms under the one rule of Jerusalem (e.g., Holladay, *Jeremiah 1*, 118; Clements, *Jeremiah*, 35). Here we see God "pulsating with passion and throbbing with pain," longing for the restoration of God's relationship with Israel, willing even to break God's own law so that love might abound (Stulmann, *Order amid Chaos*, 39). Here we see that God's love is stronger than our sin, and because God loves us so much, God is willing to do whatever is necessary to save us from sin and to restore our relationship with God, a fact that will ultimately be played out in the life, death, and resurrection of Jesus Christ.

> "Returning, as an act of inward rethinking and renewing, can lead to a blessed future only if it is a sincere and genuine returning to the Lord. It is not the inner movement of the heart that saves, but such may herald a returning to God, who can truly save." R. E. Clements, *Jeremiah*, Interpretation, 37.

As Stulmann notes, God is "undomesticated and full of pathos. Not unlike Aslan in C. S. Lewis's *The Lion, the Witch, and the Wardrobe*, Yahweh is 'wild you know. Not like a tame lion.' Indeed, Yahweh

25

defies all customary categories of control. . . . [H]e is something wild, dangerous, unfettered and free" (176). It is only in this "wildness" of God that we discover the mercy and grace that make it possible for us to repent and to know God's love in new and fresh ways.

God offers a second invitation to return (*shub*) in verse 14 with a promise to help: "I will bring you to Zion." With this invitation and announcement, we see again a glimmer of hope in the midst of judgment. It is a hope bolstered with the promise of new "shepherds" that will feed God's people with "knowledge and understanding" (v. 15). In such a time, Josiah's vision will be caught up in God's wild new work of love. Judah will be joined with Israel and they will "no longer stubbornly follow their own evil will" but "together they shall come to the land God gave to their ancestors" (vv. 17–18).

Employing the metaphor of Hosea 11, our text next likens God to a parent that has worked hard to provide for his children, a parent who hopes to pass on an inheritance to children worthy of such a loving, sacrificial gift (v. 19). But here the children don't seem to care for the father or his gifts, leaving the father with broken dreams and a broken heart.

> "The need of the hour is a 'return' to God, which denotes an inner repudiation of past disloyalty and a genuine turning back to God in repentance of heart." R. E. Clements, *Jeremiah*, Interpretation, 35.

The metaphor then shifts back to marriage, with Israel, the faithless wife leaving God, the faithful husband (v. 20). With this shift, the softer, more intimate language of God returns briefly to the language of the court, with God in the uncomfortable position of having to file suit against his guilty partner.

 Want to Know More?

About biblical metaphor? See Sallie McFague, *Metaphorical Theology* (Philadelphia: Fortress Press, 1982).

About the metaphor of Judah as a whore? See Carol A. Newsom and Sharon H. Ringe, eds., *Women's Bible Commentary*, expanded ed. (Louisville, Ky.: Westminster John Knox Press, 1998), 179–81.

A third invitation to return (*shub*) is offered in verse 22. It is preceded with an image of Israel's children weeping because they have forgotten the Lord their God (v. 21). It is an image that closely resembles Rachel's weeping for her lost children in 31:15. And so, as Holladay points out, this means "it is not the Israelites who are weeping to Yahweh, but rather that Yahweh is weeping for his lost children, the Israelites" (*Jeremiah 1*, 123).

In the latter part of verse 22 and continuing on through the rest of the chapter, we see a rare thing in the book of Jeremiah. We see a recognition of sin and an acknowledgment of guilt from Israel. She seems to recognize, if only briefly, that true salvation is only with Yahweh (v. 23). The concluding verses (vv. 24–25) read like a corporate confession of sin. Here, Israel acknowledges her lifetime of sin and the shame and dishonor it has brought her. Truly she is a shamed woman, rejected not only by her "husband" but also by "other lovers." All she can do now is wallow in her sin and misery and hope that the ways of God are somehow different from human ways.

? Questions for Reflection

1. In taking back unfaithful Judah, God seems to override his own laws. What does this action suggest regarding our treatment of other people, especially those who have offended us?
2. List and discuss as many metaphors for God as you can. What is helpful or not helpful with each one for understanding God and/or teachings about God?
3. Time and again God invites Judah to "return" to God. What does this suggest about the nature of God? What implications might this have for our relationship with others?
4. How is repentance understood in the book of Jeremiah? Does this differ in any way from the New Testament understanding of repentance? How do you understand repentance?

4 Jeremiah 6:16-21; 7:1-15

No Excuse, No Protection!

In this unit we examine the now familiar judgment of God on the people of Israel and Judah for their unwillingness to adhere to the ways of God. However, this time we look at it with the added note of problems stemming from the people's overreliance on religious ritual and tradition instead of on the God these rituals and traditions are designed to serve. Jeremiah declares that the people refuse to return to "the ancient paths" (6:16) and do not heed the warnings and teachings of Yahweh (6:17, 19). Instead, they seek "to satisfy his demands by an ever more elaborate cultus. And Yahweh will not have it" (Bright, *Jeremiah*, 50).

> "Your burnt offerings are not acceptable, nor are your sacrifices pleasing to me. Therefore thus says the LORD: See, I am laying before this people stumbling blocks against which they shall stumble; parents and children together, neighbor and friend shall perish." Jeremiah 6:20b–21.

The stubborn and foolish behavior of Judah evidenced in chapter 6 sets the stage for what follows in chapter 7 in the so-called temple sermon (see Stulmann, 40). In this sermon Jeremiah strikes out at the notion that neither the temple itself nor the various religious practices conducted there can save the people from the consuming judgment that God is about to unleash on them. He points out that burnt offerings and sacrifices are no longer pleasing to God (6:20). Furthermore, he informs them that the notion of the temple providing some sort of security in and of itself is rejected by God (7:4). As we will now see, the temple, its cultic practices, and its accompanying ideologies "are unreliable and unable to save Judah from the God who refuses to don the straightjacket of perverse and controlling systems" (Stulmann, in Diamond, O'Connor, and Stulmann, eds., *Troubling Jeremiah*, 53).

No Excuse

Our text from Jeremiah 6 begins with an admonition in verse 16: "ask for the ancient paths, where the good way lies; and walk in it." Most scholars see this as a command to find a way back to healthy community. The command may have more to do with a process, or way of living, than it does with an actual road or pathway (see, e.g., Holladay, *Jeremiah 1*, 221). Brueggemann points out that this appeal is not an attempt to return to a nostalgic "old time religion" or to "the good old days"; it is an appeal to a more radical and dangerous memory that puts an end to the false teachings and beliefs of the present (*To Pluck Up*, 70). This memory most likely refers to the ways of Moses found in the Deuteronomic laws. In any event, Judah rejects the command, no doubt because it would mean letting go of the present positions of power and prestige it enjoys in both temple and court. Judah's response is a familiar one, one that can be seen in almost any time or place, including our own. We want, and sometimes hear, a word from the Lord, but we nearly always reject that word when it conflicts with our preferred way of living.

Next comes a command to pay attention to the sentinels God provides, to "give heed to the sound of the trumpet" (v. 17). The sentinels and trumpets are sounding a warning that judgment is coming, that time is running out for those presently in power, that there is a new and terrible force about to be let loose on them and the world as punishment for neglecting the ways of God. But again, Judah rejects the command and ignores the warning. God responds by summoning the nations, the congregations, and the entire earth to hear and know what God is about to do to God's people as a result of their failure to heed God's word (vv. 18–19).

Apparently, Judah thinks that ritual nods to God are enough to secure God's favor and protection. And so Judah shows up for worship, burns a little incense, offers a few sacrifices, and then leaves, thinking all is well. But all is not well. Judah's worship routines are empty and void of meaning, which is to say they do not result in changed lives. God sees Judah's worship offerings as futile gestures unless they are accompanied by acts of justice and righteous living. Because Judah does not

> "Ultimately this deception lies in the belief that the visible institutions of religion, in this case the temple, can function in a mechanical fashion. The symbol of trust [the temple] becomes identified with the object of that faith and trust and thereby distorts and ultimately falsifies the very nature of faith itself." R. E. Clements, *Jeremiah*, Interpretation, 45–46.

engage itself in doing justice and living righteously, Jeremiah says in so many words, Don't bother with the time and expense of worship, because it is no longer pleasing or acceptable to God.

Judah, of course, turns deaf ears to the prophet's word, which is tantamount to turning deaf ears to God's word. Because of its recalcitrance, Judah has no excuse to offer that can preclude the harsh judgment about to be leveled against it.

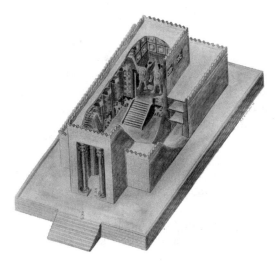

The Temple

No Protection

As mentioned previously, Judah's leadership promulgates a "theology of the temple," which sees the temple as the permanent residence of Yahweh, thus guaranteeing Yahweh's protection to all those who support the work of the temple. This theology is rooted in the claims of David and Solomon and supported by the earlier works of the psalmists (such as Ps. 132) and the prophet Isaiah (such as Isa. 37:33–35). It tends to negate the need for obedience in the lives of the faithful, and downplays the need for responsible living according to the laws of God because it fosters the belief that no matter what people do or do not do, God will protect them. According to Jeremiah, this is bad theology, the kind of theology that leads not to a better life but to a sure and certain death.

Jeremiah spends his life objecting to this kind of thinking, insisting that Yahweh is very much concerned with obedience to his word and with lives and lifestyles that honor him by just service to the wider community. The word Jeremiah delivers is that there can be no separation between love for God and love for neighbor. It should no longer surprise us to learn that Judah rejects this message. Judah still stubbornly believes that God will protect it. It falls to Jeremiah to announce that "all of Judah's sacred pillars—temple, covenant, election and Davidic dynasty—no longer provide support" (Stulmann, in Diamond, O'Connor, and Stulmann, eds. *Troubling Jeremiah*, 63).

He announces that God is about to render a swift and horrible judgment against Judah from which there will be no protection.

The Temple Sermon

The temple sermon presents us with one of the basic themes of Jeremiah's prophecies. Jeremiah is commanded "to stand in the gate of the LORD's house" and to proclaim God's word to the people of Judah (7:2). The main thrust of this prophecy is given in verses 3–4: "Amend your ways and your doings, and let me dwell with you in this place. Do not trust in these deceptive words: 'This is the temple of the LORD, the temple of the LORD, the temple of the LORD.'"

Here Jeremiah presents Judah with basically two choices. Judah can begin "walking the walk" of faith by living as God intends for it to live, or it can continue only "talking the talk" of faith, refusing to act out the faith it so glibly professes in the house of God. The first choice will lead to a longer life in the land of promise; the second choice will lead to a life of exile in the land of punishment.

Jeremiah mocks the temple liturgy with his threefold repetition of "the temple of the LORD" (v. 4). Here he speaks to the vain repetitions of the worshipers who intone the liturgy as if it were some sort of magic formula to ward off evil. The people of Judah were buying into a false sense of security and hope as if their rituals could, in and of themselves, save them. Jeremiah points out that "this deception lies in the belief that the visible institutions of religion, in this case the temple, can function in a mechanical fashion. The symbol of trust [the temple] becomes identified with the object of that faith and trust and thereby distorts and ultimately falsifies the very nature of faith itself" (Clements, 45–46). Jeremiah knows that God is far more interested in the results of worship than he is in the forms, acts, or structures of worship. In other words, God wants all of Judah to know what James will later want the church to know: Faith without works is dead (cf. James 2:14–17).

In verses 5–7, Jeremiah spells out in unmistakable terms what "walking the walk" means as opposed to simply "talking the talk." Employing the conditional form of argumentation, "if-then," he not only tells Judah what is required to assure Yahweh's continued presence with them but also argues for the more trustworthy traditions of Mosaic law (cf. Exod. 19:5) and against the less trustworthy traditions associated with David (cf. Ps. 132).

Jeremiah begins his argument by repeating his earlier charge, but this time conditionally: "*If* you amend your ways and your doings . . ." (v. 5), thus reminding Judah of Yahweh's insistence on obedience to torah. Next, he carries the conditional argument forward by recalling for Judah what obedience to torah looks like: "*if* you truly act justly one with another, *if* you do not oppress the alien, the orphan, and the widow, or shed innocent blood in this place, and *if* you do not go after other gods . . ." (vv. 5–6), in other words, *if* you really begin "walking the walk" of faith, *then* you will find favor with God and dwell with God in the land of your ancestors (v. 7).

"God is watching! And God knows the games we play. God knows how we use him and our sacred rituals to pretend all is well with us and with our relationship with God and God's world. God knows that all is not well. God knows that as soon as we get out of the doors of our sanctuaries we lay aside the things that are holy and pick up the things that are evil in God's sight. God knows that our liturgies ought to affect our ethics, but when they do not, then not even our sanctuaries can save us."

To its shame and discredit, Judah is still not interested in the walk of faith, only the talk. "Here you are, trusting in deceptive words to no avail" (v. 8). With this observation, it appears that the time for "amending" is past. Judah continues to flaunt its sin. In a series of rhetorical questions, the verdict appears all but certain: "Will you steal, murder, commit adultery, swear falsely, make offerings to Baal, and go after other gods that you have not known, and then come and stand before me in this house, which is called by my name, and say 'We are safe!'—only to go on doing all these abominations?" (vv. 9–10). The answer is certainly "yes." How incredible then that Judah should casually walk into the temple and say, "We are safe!" Nothing could be farther from the truth. The point is pushed farther: "Has this house, which is called by my name, become a den of robbers in your sight?" (v. 11a). Again, the answer is certainly "yes." "I too am watching, says the LORD" (v. 11b).

God is watching! And God knows the games we play. God knows how we use him and our sacred rituals to pretend all is well with us and with our relationship with God and God's world. God knows that all is not well. God knows that as soon as we get out of the doors of our sanctuaries we lay aside the things that are holy and pick up the things that are evil in God's sight. God knows that our liturgies ought to affect our ethics, but when they do not, then not even our sanctuaries can save us.

Jeremiah's sermon in the temple heads for its dramatic conclusion in verses 12–15. The prophet points the people's attention to Shiloh, a place they all know about, a place that had once been Israel's central sanctuary, a place where the ark of the covenant was lodged, a place where Yahweh was thought to reside, a place now vanished and gone, a place destroyed by Yahweh because of Israel's failure to keep the laws of the covenant. Go to Shiloh, says Jeremiah, and see the things that God did to it because of Israel's wickedness (v. 12). Go there and contemplate the fate of your ancestors, and see in their history a glimpse of your own future!

> ### Shiloh
>
> Shiloh was a religious center of Israel in Old Testament times. It was located about ten miles north of Bethel and is identified with the modern Khirbet Seilun. It was destroyed by the Philistines in the mid-eleventh century B.C.E.

Perhaps Judah does not see the parallel. Perhaps Judah understands the wickedness of Shiloh and the destruction that fell upon that city and its people and yet still sees Jerusalem and its people as somehow more righteous, more favored in God's eyes and therefore safe. If so, then Jeremiah is determined to correct this view. Jerusalem is no different from Shiloh; its people must obey God if they want to live and prosper. But since Jerusalem continues to disobey, breaking and mocking God's laws at every turn, so it must also be destroyed (v. 14). To make matters worse, Jeremiah announces that God's judgment against Jerusalem will be expanded to include all of Judah, an act that will lead to exile just as it had done in that earlier time for the "offspring of Ephraim" (v. 15).

What Jeremiah announces in his temple sermon is a radical new undertaking by God, namely, the destruction of God's own house and the dispersion of God's own people. There is no place and no people who can rightfully claim favor and protection from God without obedience to God's laws.

As Brueggemann says, "The parallel between Jerusalem and Shiloh invites our imaginative parallels" (*To Pluck Up*, 77). How do we disobey God's laws? How do we participate in sinful

 Want to Know More?

About the importance of the temple to ancient Jews? See R. E. Clements, *Jeremiah*, Interpretation (Atlanta: John Knox Press, 1988), 43–45; for a thorough and technical discussion, see Horst Dietrich Preuss, *Old Testament Theology*, vol. 2, Old Testament Library (Louisville, Ky: Westminster John Knox Press, 1996), 39–51.

About the city of Shiloh? See Paul J. Achtemeier, ed., *HarperCollins Bible Dictionary*, rev. ed. (New York: HarperCollins, 1996), 1014–15.

About temple theology in Old Testament Jerusalem? See Rainer Albertz, *A History of Israelite Religion in the Old Testament Period*, vol. 1 (Louisville, Ky.: Westminster John Knox Press, 1994), 132–38.

About the ark of the covenant? See Paul J. Achtemeier, ed., *HarperCollins Bible Dictionary*, rev. ed. (New York: HarperCollins, 1996), 70–71.

activities? How do we attempt to cover our sins with religious activity? How do we make idols of our worship forms and places? How do we continue to claim special favor with God?

Where are the disconnects between faith and practice? Could it be that we are just as foolish, stubborn, and mistaken as the folks in Jerusalem and Shiloh? Could it be that the message God delivered through the prophet Jeremiah is still valid for us?

? Questions for Reflection

1. A longing for the "good old days" is a universal feeling. How is it evidenced in Judah? What does Jeremiah teach regarding this longing? What are the implications for us?
2. Judah believed that the simple act of worship was, in and of itself, enough to satisfy God and ensure God's protection. According to Jeremiah, God is more interested in how worship informs and shapes one's life of service. In what ways are we like Judah? What does God want from us?
3. What is the relationship between faith and practice? List and discuss attributes of responsible living. How would you grade yourself in light of these attributes?
4. Compare and contrast life in your city or town to life in Jerusalem and Shiloh in Jeremiah's time. What might God want to say to you today?

5

No Balm in Gilead

This unit of study concerns one of the most moving and powerful passages of the book of Jeremiah, but one that, nevertheless, is surrounded by controversy. This passage is a lament, an expression of sorrow and grief that is also a genre of literature found in various books of the Bible. In the book of Jeremiah, most of the laments are attributed to the prophet himself. However, in the passage before us, there is considerable disagreement among scholars over who is speaking—Jeremiah, God, the people, or some combination of the three? The resolution of this problem is nowhere yet on the horizon. For now we will opt with O'Connor and Brueggemann and identify the speaker as God.

Seeing the speaker as God connects us with him in a new and unforgettable way, the way of the heart. Here, in contrast to the God who executes judgment and scatters his people, is the God who weeps. Here God's heart is filled with pain and grief because death can no longer be detained. Like a parent standing over the bed of a dying child, there is little left to do but grieve. And grieve God does, giving us another taste of God-with-us, aching with us and for us, even through the valley of death (cf. Ps. 23) in a way that foreshadows the saving work of Jesus Christ.

Kathleen O'Connor helps us see what it means to have a God that weeps for us:

> "My joy is gone, grief is upon me, my heart is sick. Hark, the cry of my poor people from far and wide in the land: 'Is the LORD not in Zion? Is her King not in her?'" Jeremiah 8:18–19.

To recognize that Yahweh speaks and weeps in this poem is to see a temporary but massive turning in the book. God's tears recall the broken-hearted husband, but rather than keeping him at distance as does the drama of the divorce of his wife (2:1–3:25), these poems unite Yahweh with the people in their weeping (9:17–22). God's tears mean that healing may be possible because God draws near, abandons fury, leaves aside honor, and joins the people's suffering. . . . God's tears are more powerful even than the armies under divine command because, for a poetic moment at least, God, people and cosmos articulate a common suffering and God changes sides. (Diamond, O'Connor, and Stulmann, eds. *Troubling Jeremiah*, 400–401)

This passage, along with others we will look at in unit 10, helps us to imagine the birth of a new future emerging out of the death and destruction permeating the rest of the book. God suffers with and for his people, as Jesus will later do, and out of this mutual suffering emerges a new commitment to one another, a commitment that awakens hope (see also 31:15–20).

God: Sick at Heart

In verses 19–21, we discover an interchange between God and the people. Brueggemann's suggested outline helps us to understand this interchange (see *To Pluck Up*, 88):

A   God's pain (vv. 18–19a)
B   people's question regarding God's presence (v. 19b)
C   God's question of indignation (v. 19c)
B   people's question regarding God's timing (v. 20)
A   God's pain (v. 21)

We begin in verse 18 with the deep pain God is feeling. God's joy is replaced with grief, a deep, hurting grief that makes God's heart sick. God watches as the people wander away from him, watches as they plunge deeper and deeper into sin, and watches as they play at worship, supposing that God will honor the old covenants in spite of their constant efforts to break them. God can see the pain and suffering coming to his people, and their cold indifference to it all only makes God's pain that much worse.

Next comes the question of the people: "Is the LORD not in Zion? Is her King not in her?" (v. 19b). It is a mocking statement; of course they believe the Lord is in Zion. But, as Jeremiah tries to make clear over and over again, God is withdrawing from Zion.

In the next line (v. 19c), we see again the reason for God's withdrawal from the Holy City. Judah is caught up in all kinds of idolatry, worshiping other images, while still expecting Yahweh to look upon it with favor.

Then another question arises from the people, a question of timing: "The harvest is past, the summer is ended, and we are not saved" (v. 20). This statement, together with verse 19b, suggests that Judah still expects God to be in place and on time, available when needed to protect and preserve it. It is a self-serving and foolish thought. God is not standing in the wings waiting to be rung for like an indentured servant.

This section draws to a close in the way it began—with God's deep sense of pain. God sees what the people cannot see, namely, the sin of God's people spreading like a cancer and leading them to a sure and certain death. Like a parent watching a child die, God is hurt and dismayed, and all he can do is mourn (v. 21).

> "There is a balm in Gilead to make the wounded whole. There is a balm in Gilead to heal the sin-sick soul. Sometimes I feel discouraged, and think my work's in vain, but then the Holy Spirit revives my soul again." "There Is a Balm in Gilead," from the *Presbyterian Hymnal*, #394.

No Medicine, No Physician, No Cure

In this next section, we see a haunting picture of God as a parent mourning for a sick child and wondering if there might be some new drug, some unidentified doctor out there who might yet restore the child's health. Yahweh wonders out loud if perhaps somewhere outside the city, perhaps in Gilead, there is medicine to remedy the situation. Perhaps in Gilead there is a physician who can do something to turn back the march of death. "Is there no balm in Gilead? Is there no physician there? Why then has the health of my poor people not been restored?" (v. 22).

Who does not ask such questions? Who does not search for new cures, new knowledge, new help when death comes knocking at the door? Sometimes, of course, there are other medicines and physicians who can help. But at other times there are no medicines or physicians who can help because the disease is simply too widespread, too advanced for anything or anyone to turn back. Such is the case for

> "We are accustomed to thinking about the Lord's anger and judgment but not so used to thinking about God's grief and tears. We are accustomed to thinking about God's power, the Almighty who can accomplish whatever ends by pure force. Yet, the Bible frequently knows God in a different manner—God whose strength lies in a willingness to take risks, and whose power is suffering love." John M. Bracke, *Jeremiah 1–29*, Westminster Bible Companion (Louisville, Ky.: Westminster John Knox Press, 1999), 90.

Judah. Judah is so consumed by sin, so corrupted by idolatry, that there is nothing that can save it. There is no medicine, no physician, no cure!

God's Weeping

Once it is determined that there is no cure for Judah's sickness, we see God doing what we might do in similar circumstances: God weeps! "O that my head were a spring of water, and my eyes a fountain of tears, so that I might weep day and night for the slain of my poor people!" (9:1). God's own tears are not enough to express the deep sense of loss he feels. Springs and fountains of tears are required for such deep grief.

God weeps

"O that my head were a spring of water, and my eyes a fountain of tears, so that I might weep day and night for the slain of my poor people!" Jeremiah 9:1.

"As he came near and saw the city, he wept over it, saying, 'If you, even you, had only recognized on this day the things that make for peace! But now they are hidden from your eyes. Indeed, the days will come upon you, when your enemies will set up ramparts around you and surround you, and hem you in on every side. They will crush you to the ground, you and your children within you, and they will not leave within you one stone upon another; because you did not recognize the time of your visitation from God.'" Luke 19:41–44.

As noted earlier, Jeremiah presents us with a picture of a God who is with us and for us in a way that foreshadows the work of Jesus Christ. Indeed, seeing God weeping for his people in Zion as death closes in around them is very much like the scene in Luke's Gospel when Jesus weeps over Jerusalem (Luke 19:41–44). Perhaps these tears really are more powerful than the armies of death, so that somehow, sometime, God will find a way to overcome death.

The enormity of the grief found in this passage is finally too much to handle, even for God. And so we again see God doing something we might do: God longs to get away from it all! The pain of watching his people giving themselves over to death is too much. "O that I had in the desert a traveler's lodging place, that I might leave my people and go away from them!" (v. 2). Here, like us, God wants and needs a respite, a time and a place away from all the pressures and pains of the world. The language employed is the familiar language of the psalmist, a language Jeremiah's people surely know. "O that I had wings like a dove! I would fly away and be at rest; truly, I would flee far away; I would lodge in the wilderness" (Ps. 55:6–7).

This need to get away is followed by a recitation of reasons for why God might want to break away from his people. They are adulterers, traitors, liars, and slanderers who stand for falsehood and not truth. They willingly go from one evil to another. They no longer know God.

Judah is no longer God's people. It has put aside all notions of covenant, no longer caring for any-

An oasis in the desert

body but itself. It makes a mockery of the God it supposedly worships, mouthing the temple liturgies without ever seeking to apply the words of worship to the way it lives. In effect, Judah is writing its own death certificate. Can anyone blame God for wanting to get away?

 Questions for Reflection

1. O'Connor speaks of God's tears as a source of healing. Do you agree or disagree? Why? What does this image of God convey to you?

2. Compare and contrast God's weeping over Judah with Jesus' weeping over Jerusalem in Luke 19:41–44. What do these passages say to you about God?

3. In this section of Jeremiah, it is suggested that nothing can be done to save Judah. Even God is powerless to cure its ills. What thoughts or feelings does this elicit in you? What does this suggest about the potential dangers of isolating portions of scripture from the whole?

> **Want to Know More?**
>
> **About the exile to Babylon?** See Celia Brewer Marshall, *A Guide through the Old Testament* (Louisville, Ky: Westminster John Knox Press, 1989), 108–21.
>
> **About the problem of suffering and evil?** See Shirley C. Guthrie, *Christian Doctrine*, rev. ed. (Louisville, Ky.: Westminster John Knox Press, 1994), 166–91; Tyron L. Inbody, *The Transforming God: An Interpretation of Suffering and Evil* (Louisville, Ky.: Westminster John Knox Press, 1997).

6 Jeremiah 11:18–20:18

The Confessions of Jeremiah

In this unit of study, we turn our attention to the so-called confessions of Jeremiah, which are unique in all of scripture. Nowhere else do we have such an extensive body of material reflecting the inner life of a prophet. Here we see soul-searching, heart-rendering accounts of Jeremiah's personal and spiritual struggles, all of which stem from his work as a prophet of God. The only material that comes close to expressing the kinds of feelings we will find in the confessions is found in the book of Psalms, the book of Job, and a few isolated passages regarding Moses (Exod. 17:4), Samuel (1 Sam. 15:11), Elijah (1 Kgs. 19:10), and Isaiah (Isa. 6:11; 53:68).

The confessions are scattered over ten chapters in the book of Jeremiah and do not appear in any particular order. In fact, Bright and others rearrange the confessions to better conform to their suggested time lines. However, the confessions all bear similar traits. They are autobiographical in nature. They relate to Jeremiah's sense of, and struggle with, call. They employ similar language, most often the same language God uses against the people of Israel and Judah. They express the prophet's sense of abandonment from Yahweh, who has promised him protection but who seems now to have reneged on that promise. And they all take their case directly to Yahweh, revealing the stormy relationship that exists between them.

Jeremiah is persecuted by family and friends, kings and priests, and false prophets as a result of the message he carries to them from God. Not liking the message he bears, these people try to kill the messenger. Throughout these

> "Why does the way of the guilty prosper? Why do all who are treacherous thrive?"
> Jeremiah 12:1.

various attacks on his life and person, Jeremiah maintains his innocence, and when no one else will listen, he takes his case directly to God. To our amazement, God does not always respond to him, leaving him to wonder in silent isolation about God's presence, power, and protection. And in those incidents when God does respond to him, he finds not so much comfort and reassurance as more occasions to question his vocation or call. For instance, God tells him that things will get worse instead of better (12:5–6), that God is behind the persecution (15:12), and that he, Jeremiah, needs to repent (15:19). It only stands to reason then that Jeremiah's experience of pain and suffering is deepened and made worse by the realization that his God may be behind it all.

The confessions emerge out of Jeremiah's own experience of pain and suffering at the hands of his enemies and his God; as such, they reflect the experience of pain and suffering God's people must endure. Likewise, the confessions reveal new insights into the changing relationship between God and God's people.

Like a Lamb Led to Slaughter: Jeremiah 11:18–12:6

In this confession, we see Jeremiah's growing awareness that his own people are out to get him. He likens himself to a "gentle lamb led to slaughter," innocent and unaware of his kinsmen's scheming to kill him (11:19a–b), an image that will one day be used to describe Jesus Christ and his sacrificial work (see John 1:29, 36, and numerous like references in Revelation). Now Jeremiah learns that they want to "destroy him," "cut him off from the land of the living," and see to it "that his name will no longer be remembered" (v. 19c–d). Given the nature of Jeremiah's prophecies to such people, it is not difficult to understand how they might want to find ways of silencing him.

Key Terms

Theodicy The justification of a deity's justice and goodness in light of suffering and evil.

Having given voice to his newfound situation, Jeremiah immediately moves to enlist the aid of God. After all, he is in this mess not by his own doing but by the Lord's doing. Jeremiah therefore takes his case to God with the presumption that God will honor his previous promise to protect him in his work. He also takes the request that

God will strike back at Jeremiah's enemies as just retribution for what they are attempting to do to him as God's messenger (v. 20).

God responds by identifying the people of Anathoth as those who are threatening Jeremiah with his life (v. 21). Because these people are guilty of plotting to kill God's prophet, God will punish them. Their "young men shall die by the sword; their sons and their daughters shall die by famine; and not even a remnant shall be left of them" (v. 22–23a). This "word from the Lord" serves to authenticate the prophet as God's man on the scene, and perhaps even more importantly, that the prophet's words are indeed God's words, words that need to be taken seriously.

> "Why is my pain unceasing, my wound incurable, refusing to be healed?" Jeremiah 15:18.

Questions for the Ages

Fresh with the knowledge that God will take care of his enemies, Jeremiah dares ask God the question that every person asks at some time or another: Why do the guilty prosper (12:1b)? Jeremiah places the blame squarely on God: "You plant them, and they take root; they grow and bring forth fruit" (v. 2a). Jeremiah's struggle with this question of theodicy has a contemporary ring to it. If God is really in charge of the world, if God is really sovereign over all things, then God must also be responsible in some way for the prospering of the wicked. If God is really interested in justice, then why does he bring prosperity to the very ones that speak and work against God?

These are indeed questions for the ages, questions that our text does not answer in any satisfactory way. And so we find Jeremiah moving on in his argument with God. "You, O LORD, know me; you see me and test me—my heart is with you" (v. 3a). Here Jeremiah pleads his own righteousness. His heart is with God, leading him to do only those things God wants him to do. Affirming his righteousness before the righteousness of God, he dares to suggest that there are others who should, like sheep, rightly be led to the slaughter (v. 3b). To support his suggestion, Jeremiah points to the drought and the effects it is having on other inno-

> "Whatever else might be said about the Bible, it is nothing if not honest when it comes to describing the costly nature of God's work."

cent creatures, a drought he believes is caused by the sins of the wicked (v. 4).

God's response to Jeremiah is a shocking one, even to us. In effect, God says to Jeremiah, You haven't seen anything yet! Instead of offering reassuring words, God spins a scary story of terrifying dimensions. "If you have raced with foot-runners and they have wearied you, how will you compete with horses? And if in a safe land you fall down, how will you fare in the thickets of the Jordan?" (v. 5). God is telling Jeremiah that there are far worse things to come than what he has already experienced.

God caps off this unusual response with a warning that most surely adds to Jeremiah's struggle: Don't believe your family when they cozy up to you with kind words, because, like the others in your hometown, they too are out to get you (v. 6)!

Why do the evil prosper? It is still an unanswered question. As Brueggemann points out, "Yahweh's response is not unlike the whirlwind speech of Job 38–41, which simply overrides the problem of theodicy" (*To Pluck Up*, 115). We are left with the questions raised earlier concerning God's sovereignty and justice. With Jeremiah, all we can do is press on with the work God gives us to do, trusting that God will somehow be with us.

Why Was I Born? Jeremiah 15:10–21

In this confession, we find Jeremiah in a deep depression, ruing the day he was born (v. 10a). Jeremiah is caught between two worlds— the world of his people, who no longer pay any attention to him or his message, and the world of his God, who keeps insisting that Jeremiah continue delivering his harsh message no matter what it might cost him personally to do so. Understandably, Jeremiah cries out in pain to God, trying to make a case for himself: "I have not lent, nor have I borrowed," the kinds of activities that often cause quarrels, "yet all of them curse me" (v. 10b). In his mind, his suffering and pain is unwarranted. He isn't doing the kinds of things his countrymen are doing; he only does what God wants him to do. So, he wonders, why must I suffer so? It is a good question, a question that speaks to the costly nature of discipleship.

The response Jeremiah receives from Yahweh is a strange one. Once again, Yahweh points to God's own role in the mess. "I have imposed enemies on you in a time of trouble and in a time of distress"

(v. 11). Here Yahweh seems to say that Jeremiah's troubles are a natural part of the terrible message he bears. As God's man on the scene,

Jeremiah will suffer the same sorts of things all Judah will suffer: His wealth will be given as plunder, and he will have to serve his enemies in a land he doesn't know (vv. 13–14). So, in a real sense, the troubles he is presently experiencing serve to foreshadow the troubles he and all of Judah will experience in the coming judgment. As Brueggemann puts it, "The role of Jeremiah is lost in the overriding decision of Yahweh against Jerusalem, Judah and the land. There is not a hint of vindication or comfort for the prophet" (*To Pluck Up*, 139).

Why does God allow suffering?

In spite of the less than satisfactory answer Jeremiah gets from Yahweh, he tries again. "O LORD, you know . . ." (v. 15a). What is Jeremiah referring to? Perhaps he means to put God on the spot. God knows what is happening in his life, so why isn't God doing something about it? Jeremiah asks God to "remember" him, to "visit" him, to "bring down retribution" on his enemies, and to not be taken away (v. 15). He reminds God that the pain he feels is due to the work God gave him to do; so, in a very real sense, it is God's fault that he suffers (v. 15b). Jeremiah reminds God how he delights in God's word and how he has steadfastly refused to join the company of the wicked (vv. 16–17). And then he really lets loose: "Why is my pain unceasing, my wound incurable, refusing to be healed? Truly, you are to me like a deceitful brook, like waters that fail" (v. 18).

"Truly this was one of the great turning-points that prophecy underwent during the biblical period. Jeremiah's success as a prophet was not to be measured by the extent to which he had been able to persuade his hearers to listen to the word of God and thereby avoid whatever dangers faced them, but rather in the firmness and consistency with which he bore testimony to the righteous purpose and grand design of God." R. E. Clements, *Jeremiah*, Interpretation, 123–24.

Here Jeremiah accuses Yahweh of being unreliable and untrustworthy. In Jeremiah's mind, Yahweh has either forgotten Yahweh's promises to Jeremiah, or has changed his mind. Either way, Jeremiah doesn't like it, and he tells God so in no uncertain terms. Jeremiah doesn't hesitate to give voice to his feelings, even those that seem dark and foreboding. Perhaps we can learn something from his example.

Finally, Jeremiah gets something of the answer he is looking for, but with conditions: "*If* you turn back, I will take you back. . . . *If* you utter what is precious, and not what is worthless, you shall serve as my mouth" (v. 19a–b). God suggests that, like Judah, Jeremiah needs to repent, to reorient himself to covenant living, to give himself completely to his work no matter what it may cost him, for that is the only way he can enjoy God's presence and protection. If Jeremiah does these things, then he need not worry about anything, his fate or his people's fate, for the people will turn to God (v. 19c).

This confession closes with words of reassurance remarkably similar to the words at the end of chapter 1. Here Yahweh unconditionally reaffirms and recommits to his promise of protection for Jeremiah: "I am with you to save you and deliver you . . . and redeem you" (vv. 20c–21).

Jeremiah begins this confession by cursing the day he was born, because his life's work is bringing him nothing but trouble and pain. Not only is he rejected and despised by his countrymen, he also seems to be neglected by God. The real question lurking behind this confession is whether or not Yahweh will support his messenger as well as his message. The closing verses indicate that the answer is "yes," God will support his messenger. Perhaps this vow of support is an indicator of the support God will one day give to Judah. If so, this isolated experience of Jeremiah might foreshadow the exile experience of Judah.

Be Not a Terror: Jeremiah 17:14–18

In Psalter-like language, Jeremiah petitions Yahweh to heal and to save him (v. 14). He has tried to repent, he has puzzled over the nature of his call and done his best to be faithful to that call, and still his personal situation is full of pain and suffering. He tries now to do precisely what Judah is failing to do: He tries to throw himself on the mercy of Yahweh. Jeremiah is terrified to the point of breaking, and so he prays to Yahweh: "Do not become a terror to me; you are my refuge" (v. 17).

Jeremiah also reveals the taunting work of his adversaries: "See how they say to me, 'Where is the word of the LORD?'" (v. 15). Such taunting and ridicule, however, hasn't kept him from doing his job: "I have not run away from being a shepherd in your service" (v. 16a). He also points out his abiding concern for his people, hoping that they would amend their ways and be spared the awful judgment about to be carried out: "nor have I desired the fatal day" (v. 16b).

But now, it seems, the personal pressure has become too much for him to bear. The people of Judah continue to support the beliefs of the false prophets who say that all is well, that Jerusalem and the temple are safe from harm's way. Consequently, they continue to break the laws of the covenant. Jeremiah's words seem to be ignored by the people and by God. In desperation, Jeremiah asks Yahweh to let the fatal blow fall: "Let my persecutors be shamed, . . . let them be dismayed . . . ; bring on them the day of disaster; destroy them with double destruction!" (v. 18).

Something appears to be changed in Jeremiah. What he now wants more than anything else is to have his words validated by God's actions so that he will no longer be shamed or dismayed (see v. 18). But Jeremiah is left hanging in suspense. And so are we. There is no word from Yahweh!

Caught in a Pit: Jeremiah 18:18–23

Once again we see the personal sufferings of Jeremiah. Jeremiah is persecuted beyond belief by his own people, the very people he was trying to save by sharing Yahweh's word with them. But Yahweh's word is different from what they want to hear, and so they reject it and try to silence that word by doing away with the one who speaks it. In this confession, we have a picture of a man broken in spirit, crying out for God to avenge him by striking back at the people who are persecuting him.

Jeremiah's enemies are powerful and persistent. They pledge themselves not to listen to his words, and they plot against him to silence him from ever speaking again. They assume that he is a traitor, someone who no longer supports court or temple policy, someone who doesn't think Judah can prevail against her enemies. Indeed, Jeremiah is opposed to court and temple policies and he believes that Judah will not prevail against her enemies, but he is not the traitor they claim he is. To the contrary, he only wants to help them.

Jeremiah continues to level the charge that Judah is failing to keep covenant with God and neglecting God's message to amend her behavior. That charge is threatening to the rulers of the establishment, and so they plot against him (v. 18).

In response to this known plot, Jeremiah appeals to God for help. He notes his role as mediator, as one who has tried "to speak good for them, to turn away your wrath from them" (v. 20b). But now he is ready for God to deliver the judgment God has promised: "Give their children over to famine; hurl them out to the power of the sword, let their wives become childless and widowed. May their men meet death by pestilence, their youths be slain by the sword. . . .You, O LORD, know all their plotting to kill me. Do not forgive their iniquity, do not blot out their sin from your sight" (vv. 21–23).

Here Jeremiah pleads for justice without any sense of mercy. He asks God to be just and righteous toward him, who has done no wrong, and to be just and righteous toward his enemies, who do nothing right. The main issue behind this confession seems to be the validity of the judgment Jeremiah is called to announce against Judah and Jerusalem. The plotting against Jeremiah merely represents the greater problem of the plotting against Yahweh. It is this greater problem that will bring death and destruction to Judah.

> "Wretched man that I am! Who will rescue me from this body of death?" Romans 7:24.

A Laughingstock: Jeremiah 20:7–18

Any good preacher or prophet worth his salt wants to be heard and taken seriously. Jeremiah is no different. He desperately wants his people to listen to him, to take what he says seriously, to learn from God and thus be spared the pain of judgment and a life lived in exile. But his people are unresponsive to his message and hostile toward him. They beat him and put him in stocks, humiliating him in front of the world (20:2). This act sets the stage for the final and most agonizing personal confession Jeremiah makes.

Jeremiah undoubtedly feels damned if he does and damned if he doesn't when it comes to delivering God's message (vv. 8–9). If he delivers the message, he only brings more pain and suffering upon himself. If he doesn't deliver the message, he risks paying an even bigger price at the hands of God. Instead of turning away from God and further isolating himself, as we might do in similar circumstances, Jeremiah engages God and "spills his guts" in a way that is unparalleled in all the Bible. In the end, he articulates the existential question every person must ask: Why was I born? (v. 18).

In this confession, Jeremiah feels victimized not only by his peers but, more importantly, by his God: "O LORD, you have enticed me, . . . overpowered me. . . . [Your word] has become for me a reproach and derision all day long" (vv. 7–8; cf. Job 9:16–19). When Jeremiah speaks, Yahweh does not back him up. When Jeremiah is silent, Yahweh does not comfort him. Yahweh is the one who got Jeremiah into this awful mess and yet does nothing to help him get out of it.

The existential crisis Jeremiah experiences is quite similar to that of the apostle Paul: "I delight in the law of God in my inmost self, but I see in my members another law at war with the law of my mind, making me captive to the law of sin that dwells in my members. Wretched man that I am! Who will rescue me from this body of death?" (Rom. 7:22–24) For Paul, the answer is Jesus Christ (Rom. 7:25a). For Jeremiah, the answer comes in verse 13: "Praise the LORD! For he has delivered the life of the needy from the hands of evildoers." Even so, God's answer comes when God is ready and not necessarily when we want or need it. In Jeremiah's case, the judgment he is looking for does not come for a long time, leaving him in a constant vocational crisis.

Even though speaking God's word brings him nothing but agony, Jeremiah can't help but speak it because it is like a burning fire, shut up in his bones, a fire he cannot hold in (v. 9). The word of God heaps terror not only upon Judah but upon Jeremiah, stirring up people to denounce him and seek revenge on him for speaking out against the state (v. 10). Knowing, intellectually at least, that God is fighting with him (v. 11), he again asks God to unleash a just and fitting retribution on his enemies (v. 12b), but God doesn't seem to answer his request, leaving Jeremiah to sink deeper and deeper into despair: "Cursed be the day on which I was born! . . . Cursed be the man who brought the news to my father, . . . because he did not kill me in the womb; so my mother would have been my grave. . . . Why did I come forth from the womb to see toil and sorrow, and spend my days in shame?" (vv. 14–18).

Whatever else might be said about the Bible, it is nothing if not honest when it comes to describing the costly nature of God's work. If Jeremiah is any indication, faithfulness to God and to one's vocation does not necessarily lead one to happiness; indeed, it often leads to intense suffering and deep despair. Yet despair is not necessarily an enemy to faith. It can be, and often is, a pathway to spiritual growth and understanding. As Kierkegaard explains in *The Sickness unto Death*, "the greater degree of consciousness, the more intense the despair" (42), suggesting that despair, in causing a person to lose the desire to live to herself, may lead that person to find her fundamental identity as a child of God. In despairing his life, in "losing his life," Jeremiah finds something of far greater importance and value.

The personal dilemma of Jeremiah and the full measure of what it teaches finds its fullest expression in the words and acts of Jesus: "If any want to become my followers, let them deny themselves and take up their cross and follow me. For those who want to save their life will lose it, and those who lose their life for my sake will find it. For what will it profit them if they gain the whole world but forfeit their life?" (Matt. 16:24–26). These words are even more poignant when one realizes that even Jesus had to give up his life, literally and figuratively, in order to find his true identity and vocation.

As Clements rightly suggests, the confession of Jeremiah provides "one of the great turning-points that prophecy underwent in the biblical period. Jeremiah's success was not to be measured by the extent to which he had been able to persuade his hearers to listen to the word of God . . . , but rather in the firmness and consistency with which he bore testimony to the righteous purpose and grand design of God . . . who is to be regarded as the Creator of the universe, the Source and Ground of righteousness, justice, and truth" (123–24). Certainly the "success" of Jesus could be judged in the same way.

Jeremiah asks the question of the ages: Why was I born? The answer he gets here and elsewhere also seems to be for the ages: to bring glory to God by being faithful to one's call.

Want to Know More?

About the confessions of Jeremiah? See Donald E. Gowan, *Theology of the Prophetic Books* (Louisville, Ky.: Westminster John Knox Press, 1998), 107–9; *The Access Bible* (New York: Oxford University Press, 1999), 987.

About theodicy? See C. S. Lewis, *The Problem of Pain* (New York: HarperCollins, 2001); Shirley C. Guthrie, *Christian Doctrine*, rev. ed. (Louisville, Ky.: Westminster John Knox Press, 1994), 166–91; Tyron L. Inbody, *The Transforming God: An Interpretation of Suffering and Evil* (Louisville, Ky.: Westminster John Knox Press, 1997).

About the theological concept of suffering? See Alan Richardson and John Bowden, eds. *The Westminster Dictionary of Christian Theology* (Philadelphia: Westminster Press, 1983), 555–56.

? Questions for Reflection

1. Jeremiah suggests that God is the author of pain and suffering. Do you agree or disagree? Why?

2. Jeremiah, like Jesus after him, is likened to a sacrificial lamb. Why? What are the implications for Jeremiah and for us?

3. In light of God's sovereignty and power, how do you explain the existence of evil?

4. How might the confessions of Jeremiah speak to us in our times of distress and depression? How can experiences of pain and suffering draw us closer to God and to each other?

Prophetic Signs

The prophets of Israel often articulated and/or performed certain acts that served as signs or symbols to reveal something about Yahweh and/or Yahweh's people. In many instances, these signs served to bring about the very thing they were designed to reveal. In this unit, we look at three such signs and how they function in Jeremiah's prophetic work.

A Loincloth: Jeremiah 13:1-11

As we have noted in previous units, Israel and Judah are under the judgment of Yahweh for having violated their covenant with him. In chapter 13, this violation and judgment is acted out in the parable-like story of the loincloth.

Yahweh commands Jeremiah to buy and wear a loincloth (v. 1). After some period of time, he tells Jeremiah to take it off, go to the river Euphrates, and hide the loincloth in the cleft of a rock (v. 2). Then, after many days, Jeremiah is told to go back to the Euphrates and dig up the loincloth, which, of course, was rotten and "good for nothing" (vv. 6–7).

As in most such stories, we need not concern ourselves too much with the details. They may very well have been made up to help make a point. For instance, most scholars doubt that Jeremiah actually made two trips to the river Euphrates, a trip of several hundred miles. Even if he did, most of its banks were void of rocks where one might hide something like a loincloth. It is more likely that those who recorded this sign had in mind a wadi just north of Anathoth called

Parah, which in Hebrew has a similar spelling and sound as the word for Euphrates (*parata* and *perata,* respectively). In any case, the meaning of the story is clear.

In verses 8–11, Yahweh provides his interpretation to this sign. The loincloth represents Judah and Jerusalem, people now seen as evil in Yahweh's sight because of their refusal to hear God's word and their constant pursuit of other gods. Like the rotten loincloth, they are now "good for nothing."

The loincloth is rich in symbolism. It is, of course, among the most personal and private pieces of clothing. It is meant to cling to and support the person for whom it is purchased, and therefore it is a garment that needs regular attention in order to be kept clean and useful for its intended purpose. It is meant to be worn and used, not hidden away somewhere.

> "The symbol provides a place where spiritual and material come together. It arouses an awareness of God and God's will or purpose. For example, the law, the land, the covenant, and the Temple are symbols of God's electing grace. They are things present and visible that represent things transcendent or invisible, namely, God's electing grace and Israel's response of obedience." Paul J. Achtemeier, ed., *HarperCollins Bible Dictionary,* rev. ed., 1076.

This story raises the question of whether or not God would reject and disown God's own covenant people. The answer is a qualified "yes." If his people failed to cling to God, to keep themselves clean from sin and useful for his work, if they continued in their refusal to hear God's word and continued to chase after other gods so as to defile and soil themselves to the point of being useless to God, then yes, God would reject and disown them and allow them to self-destruct.

This sign portrays the entire history of Israel, both in the way it points to Israel's intended relationship to God, and in the way it points to Israel's constant betrayal of that relationship, thus becoming "good for nothing." It also raises a question that Christians continue to struggle with, a question Paul first posed to the people of Corinth: "Do you not know . . . that you are not your own? For you were bought with a price; therefore glorify God" (1 Cor. 6:19–20).

While from the perspective of the entire biblical record we might question whether or not God would actually desert us, certainly we would do well to ask ourselves if we are useful to God in any real and tangible way. Do we endeavor to cling to him, to do our part to maintain an intimate and personal relationship with him? Do we endeavor to glorify him by giving ourselves in service to his people? These are questions that will not go away, questions that deal with the core realities of the faith we so glibly confess.

A Broken Jug: Jeremiah 19

In chapter 19 we find Yahweh commanding Jeremiah to combine in public words and actions his message to Judah and Jerusalem. This sign involves an earthenware jug, perhaps playing off of the story of the potter's house in the preceding chapter. Here Jeremiah is commanded to purchase a jug and then to head out the Potsherd Gate to deliver a message to some of the elders and senior priests (vv. 1–2). The Potsherd Gate may refer more precisely to the Dung Gate; the reference is to a place of refuse, or the dump, or the landfill, as we might now call it. Once in place, he engages in a little street theater, joining speech with actions and movements.

> "This action [the breaking of the pot] fits into a known and widely attested pattern of similar actions employed to convey the divine word. It is a form of street theatre, but with a far more serious purpose than merely to attract attention and entertain. The action both dramatized and served to give visual impact to the coming action of God." R. E. Clements, *Jeremiah*, Interpretation, 118.

The words he delivers are once again words of impending doom. God is about to bring disaster upon all the people because of their idolatry (vv. 3–5). The people have forsaken Yahweh and profaned his city with offerings and sacrifices to Baal, activities unimaginable even to Yahweh (vv. 4–5). Jeremiah tells the people that the valley they are looking over will be renamed the valley of Slaughter because they will all be killed and their dead bodies thrown out as food for the birds and wild animals (vv. 6–7). It is a horrifying picture of hellish proportions.

Then, to bring even more clarity to this grisly word from the Lord, Jeremiah is told to break the earthenware jug he had earlier purchased, thus providing a visual aid to the words of interpretation that follow. With the image of the broken jug now fresh in everyone's mind, Jeremiah delivers Yahweh's interpretation of this action: "I will break this people and this city, as one breaks a potter's vessel, so that it can never be mended. In Topheth they shall bury until there is no more room to bury" (v. 10).

This word of the Lord stands in contradiction to the commonly held beliefs of Judah and Jerusalem. They wrongly believe that Yahweh will protect and preserve them no matter what they do or don't do. They think they have a deal with God that cannot be broken. No wonder they have such a hard time hearing what Jeremiah has to say.

Jeremiah's use of a prop to help get the people's attention does not work. The people keep right on doing what they had been doing, giving themselves to the practice of other religions. So Jeremiah returns to the temple court and announces yet another time the word of the Lord: "I am now bringing upon this city and upon all its towns all the disaster that I have pronounced against it, because they have stiffened their necks, refusing to hear my words" (v. 15).

> "Thus says the LORD of hosts: So will I break this people and this city, as one breaks a potter's vessel, so that it can never be mended. In Topheth they shall bury until there is no more room to bury." Jeremiah 19:11.

The final indictment Jeremiah pronounces here is a familiar one: The people have refused to listen to God's word. As Brueggemann so profoundly puts it,

> Everything depends on listening. Everyone suffers when there is no listening. . . . Not listening is the fundamental act of autonomy and bad faith. Not to listen is not to belong, not to concede sovereignty. Not listening is to claim one's own place and take one's own counsel. It is to imagine one is free to order life as one wills. . . . Even Jerusalem in its splendor and dignity is not so free, so autonomous. Such a mistaken pretense leads only to death. (*To Pluck Up,* 171)

Sadly, Jerusalem does not listen and so paves the way to her death.

Even now, in the twenty-first century, we have a problem listening to God. We fail to concede to God's sovereignty. We refuse to listen to God's word, especially when it contradicts our own words. Could it be that Jeremiah's prophecy regarding Judah is also relevant for us?

A Field: Jeremiah 32:6–25

In chapter 32 we come upon a sign that marks a major shift in Jeremiah's prophetic work and articulates the central message of the "Little Book of Consolation," a portion of the book of Jeremiah to be addressed in unit 10. The people of Judah are in absolute turmoil. The Babylonians have arrived and are laying siege to Jerusalem. Egypt is rattling its swords and threatening to invade from the south. Jeremiah is under house arrest, and at long last, his prophecies are beginning to be fulfilled right before everyone's eyes. Yet, right when all appears to be lost, a new word comes to Jeremiah, a word he and his people can hardly believe.

Yahweh instructs Jeremiah to buy a field in his home town of Anathoth (v. 7). Next, Jeremiah's cousin, Hanamel, comes to him and asks him to exercise his right of possession by purchasing the field he (Hanamel) owns in Anathoth. This is a sign of confirmation for Jeremiah, for then he "knew that this was the word of the LORD" (v. 8).

> "This sign is incredible. It points to an almost unimaginable future. Here, in the face of immediate exile, Jeremiah buys land."

The next several verses outline the legal purchase of that land according to the law codes of Leviticus 25. The purchase is made "decently and in order," and in the presence of witnesses so that, in the future, there can be no question about the legality of this purchase. The deed is given to Baruch for safekeeping, the first mention of the one who will later be identified as the scribe who commits Jeremiah's prophecies to writing (vv. 9–14).

This sign is incredible. It points to an almost unimaginable future. Here, in the face of immediate exile, Jeremiah buys land. This prophet of bad news goes on record to suggest that there will be life after exile and, in doing so, becomes a prophet of good news for all of Judah.

The meaning of this sign is articulated by Yahweh in verse 15: "Houses and fields and vineyards shall again be bought in this land." Here God himself announces that judgment and exile are not the last words.

This good news from Yahweh prompts Jeremiah to pray (v. 17–25). Basking in the glow of this newfound hope, the prophet affirms Yahweh as the maker of heaven and earth, and then boldly affirms that nothing is too hard for God. Yahweh, he notes, is the God of steadfast love, love that extends across time to all generations. Then the prophet recalls some of the seemingly impossible things God has already done: signs and wonders in Egypt, the deliverance of Israel from Egypt, the gift of a land flowing with milk and honey. Next, he notes the sin of Israel, its people's failure to follow God's law, and the judgments they endure as punishment for their sins. He points to the siege-ramps presently laid against Jerusalem and the horrible things about to happen to it. Then the prophet concludes his prayer with a resounding note of hope: "Yet you, O Lord GOD, have said to me, 'Buy the field for money and get witnesses'" (v. 25).

With this new command, hope is unleashed on a people who have no hope. Here we see that there is indeed nothing that is too hard for

"In deciding to purchase the field at Anathoth, Jeremiah took a step of faith. . . . In doing so, he perceived that his action had taken on a sacramental significance as a sign more widely relevant concerning God's future intentions for his people." R. E. Clements, *Jeremiah*, Interpretation, 194.

Want to Know More?

About symbols in the Old Testament? See Paul J. Achtemeier, ed., *HarperCollins Bible Dictionary*, rev. ed. (New York: Harper-Collins, 1996), 1076–79.

About the law codes of Leviticus 25? See Martin Noth, *Leviticus*, Old Testament Library (Philadelphia: Westminster Press, 1977), 181–93.

God to do. Yahweh—the God who created the heavens and the earth, the one who brought the promise of children to a barren old woman, the one who led Israel out of Egypt—is the one who can and will bring about new life. This, then, is the hope that will sustain Judah in exile. Truly it is a hope worth investing in!

This sign is a reminder that there is nothing we can do to thwart God's purposes. God is sovereign and free to do whatever he wills to do. And God wills life for the people of God, even life beyond exile and death. This is the hope that sustains Jeremiah and Judah in exile. For present-day Christians, this is the hope realized in the resurrection of Jesus Christ.

? Questions for Reflection

1. The loincloth sign suggests the possibility of God disowning his people. Do you think God would do that? Why or why not?
2. The loincloth sign also suggests that God's people owe God something. Do you agree or disagree? What do we owe God?
3. Brueggemann suggests that "not listening" is an act of autonomy and bad faith. What do you think he means by that, and what are the implications for us?
4. How does the purchase of land in Anathoth serve the people in exile? What are the implications for us? How might this sign relate to the death and resurrection of Jesus Christ?

The Folly of Kings and False Prophets

We turn our attention now to Jeremiah's prophecies concerning the kings and false prophets of Judah. The primary purpose of the monarchy is to do justice and to care for the needy (21:12; cf. Exod. 22:20–23). The primary purpose of prophets is to deliver the word of the Lord. In Jeremiah's view, the kings and prophets of his day are not fulfilling their purposes; they serve only themselves and therefore lead the people of Judah away from Yahweh. The chapters now before us give us a good picture of Jeremiah's message to the kings and prophets and his understanding of their role in the downfall of Judah.

Zedekiah's Folly

Chapter 21 opens with a surprising note: King Zedekiah is asking Jeremiah for advice and counsel! Judah is staring disaster in the face. The armies of Babylon are tightening their grip. The king, seeing the handwriting on the wall, is greatly troubled. He is now grasping at straws, looking for help wherever and however he can get it. He dispatches emissaries to Jeremiah who ask the prophet to seek the Lord's help in turning back Judah's adversaries (vv. 1–2).

In light of Yahweh's covenant history with his people, the king's request is a logical one. And in light of the role of the prophet to provide for the welfare of God's people, the king can expect a favorable answer. But Jeremiah is not like other prophets. The word he brings from the Lord is not a word of comfort and support but a word of judgment: "I am going to turn back the weapons of war that are in your hands and with which you are fighting against the king of Babylon. . . .

I myself will fight against you with outstretched hand and mighty arm, in anger, in fury, and in great wrath" (vv. 4–5). Here Jeremiah turns the king's request upside down. The language of covenant history, heretofore used in the deliverance of God's people, is now used in the destruction of God's people. The "turning back" and "striking down" is now directed toward Judah and not her enemies. Indeed, the "outstretched hand" and "mighty arm" of Yahweh is a much bigger threat to the king and his kingdom than the mighty armies of Babylon.

Key Terms

Remnant Mainly found in the prophetic books, this word refers to the portion of the nation of Israel that remained faithful to God.

In verses 11–14, we are reminded of why Yahweh has turned against the king. The duties of a monarch include executing justice and delivering all those who are oppressed. This king, like others before him, is not living up to his calling. In fact, he uses and exploits God's people to prop up his corrupt policies. For him, there can be no escape from Yahweh's judgment: "I am against you. . . . I will punish you according to the fruit of your doings. . . . I will kindle a fire in its forest, and it shall devour all that is around it" (vv. 13–14).

Jehoiakim's Folly

Chapter 22 speaks to the mistaken notion that the mere presence of the "house of David" is a guarantee of Yahweh's protection. Again, it is easy to understand why the king and his advisors believed in God's protection. After all, this very God had authorized the monarchy and promised to preserve it, a promise that by this time had endured for over three hundred years. But to Jeremiah's way of thinking, the problem with this notion is its focus on the institution of the monarchy as opposed to a focus on the God the monarchy is supposed to serve. "Any king who indulged in oppression and abused the privileges of his position could not expect to receive the divine blessing and support" (Clements, 130). Jeremiah brings God's warning to the king: "Act with justice and righteousness. . . . [I]f you will not heed these words, I swear by myself, says the LORD, that this house shall become a desolation" (vv. 3–5).

This already severe and shocking word is sharpened even more in verses 13–19. Here Jeremiah points specifically to King Jehoiakim's tyrannical and oppressive methods of feathering his own nest: "Woe to him who builds his house by unrighteousness, . . . who makes his neighbors work for nothing, . . . who says, 'I will build myself a spacious house . . . , paneling it with cedar, and painting it with vermilion" (vv. 13–14). The king treats his people as slaves, as if they were already exiled, forcing them to work without wage simply to build himself a larger, more spectacular house.

Jeremiah continues his charge against Jehoiakim by comparing him to his father, Josiah, the one king of Judah who attempted to serve the Lord and his people: "Did not your father eat and drink and do justice and righteousness? Then it was well with him. He judged the cause of the poor and needy. . . . But your eyes and heart are only on your dishonest gain, for shedding innocent blood, and for practicing oppression and violence" (vv. 15–17). With these words, Jeremiah levels perhaps the most condemning words in all of the Bible. Because of the king's dishonesty and corruption he will be "dragged off and thrown out beyond the gates of Jerusalem" (v. 19).

> "Any king who indulged in oppression and abused privileges of his position could not expect to receive the divine blessing and support. God had certainly not given Jehoiakim, or in fact any member of the royal house, the freedom to do only as he pleased. If the kings became oppressors—even the kings of the Davidic line—they could indeed be removed from their high office. . . . The relationship of the kingship to God—even that of the kingship of David's line—did not guarantee Israel or Judah, which had remained loyal to the Davidic dynasty, an unlimited assurance of God's protection." R. E. Clements, *Jeremiah*, Interpretation, 130–31.

Jehoiachin's Folly

The last king Jeremiah goes after in this unit is Jehoichin, the son of Jehoiakim, who died while Jerusalem was under siege. Jehoichin's reign lasted only three months, after which he was exiled to Babylon (see 2 Kgs. 24:8, 15).

This prophecy likens Jehoiachin to Yahweh's signet ring, a royal symbol of power and authority. The ring is torn off Yahweh's hand and given to another king, Nebuchadrezzar. Jehoiachin is also compared to a broken pot, which is thrown away because it is no longer useful. To make matters worse, there is no one to succeed him to the throne of David (see vv. 24–30).

Jeremiah's message could not be clearer. The "house of David" is to be destroyed without any hope of restoration. The monarchy has failed to fulfill its purpose and, in doing so, has failed Yahweh and

Yahweh's people. This failure has wide-ranging consequences. The old regimes of court and temple will no longer be able to stand up against Judah's adversaries. The people they are charged to look after and care for will be scattered and sold into slavery. Even the so-called promised land will dry up and die. The seeds of sin sown by the king and his cohorts have sprouted and grown and overtaken a once beautiful garden. Life for Judah would never again be the same.

The False Prophets' Folly

As we will now see in chapter 23, the kings are not the only ones to blame for Judah's demise. The other competing prophets also contribute to the problem. These other prophets are essentially puppets for power-hungry leaders of temple and court. Rather than look for and share the word of the Lord, these prophets dishonor the Lord with their corrupt worship rituals. Jeremiah refers to them as adulterers because of their unfaithfulness to Yahweh. Rather than upholding the old Mosaic laws, they incorporate pagan rituals with their own. Most probably these pagan rites involve some of the sexual fertility practices used in the worship of Baal (see Clements, 140–41). Such rites are designed as a means for ensuring new fruits from the land and from the people. But according to Jeremiah, all such designs are fruitless; they bring about nothing but destruction and death: "For the land is full of adulterers; because of the curse the land mourns, and the pastures of the wilderness are dried up" (v. 10).

> "The 'false' prophets were the representatives of a national faith in salvation." Horst Dietrich Preuss, *Old Testament Theology*, vol. 2, 85.

The sins of these false prophets are a special abomination in God's sight. These prophets do not know the way of the Lord, or if they do, they ignore it in order to please their superiors and keep their jobs. Jeremiah announces a special judgment on them. They are to be driven to dark and slippery paths where they will fall victim to disaster (v. 12). The message is quite clear: Even the "religious" cannot escape God's judgment.

A second incident of adultery is cited in verse 14: These prophets walk in lies and strengthen the hands of evildoers so that no one turns from wickedness; they have become like Sodom and Gomorrah. Because of their sin, these prophets will soon be made to eat wormwood and drink poisoned water (v. 15). In other words, their sin is going to catch up with them and consume them.

Another charge Jeremiah levels against the false prophets is that "they speak visions of their own minds, not from the mouth of the LORD. They keep saying to those who despise the word of the LORD, 'It shall be well with you';

Jerusalem

and to all who stubbornly follow their own stubborn hearts, they say, 'No calamity shall come upon you'" (vv. 16–17). Theirs is a self-serving theology, a theology designed to please the power brokers of temple and court, a theology based perhaps on the mistaken notion that God would preserve the monarchy and protect the temple. These prophets do not serve the truth and they do not serve Yahweh.

The truth is, judgment is coming on all the people of Judah, a judgment that will specifically target the rulers of court and temple. The old centers of power will be dismantled and destroyed. And, adding insult to injury, Yahweh is the one who will bring it all about. "Look," says Jeremiah, "the storm of the LORD! Wrath has gone forth, a whirling tempest; it will burst upon the head of the wicked. The anger of the LORD will not turn back until he has executed and accomplished the intents of his mind" (vv. 19–20). These false prophets speak only the good news "of their own minds," but the truth is, God's consuming judgment will blow over all of Judah until God accomplishes "the intents of his mind."

> "False prophecy is a threat to the integrity of the true prophet and serves to undermine the force and clarity with which the word of God is heard. . . . Only a sensitive and morally alert understanding of the nature of God, awake also to the facts of the contemporary religious and political scene, could hope to recognize the true prophet from the false." R. E. Clements, *Jeremiah, Interpretation,* 143.

This conflict raises one of the most perplexing problems of any age: How do we distinguish what is of God's mind and what is simply the wishes of our own minds? As we have seen in earlier chapters, it is a problem Jeremiah struggled with for most of his ministry because the people wanted to believe the better news of kings and other prophets and not the more difficult news of Jeremiah, whose

61

prophecies went unfulfilled for a long time. Is it only in hindsight that we can rightly discern the word of the Lord, or is there some way to see it now? (see Deut. 13:1–5; 18:15–22; and Clements, 143).

Yahweh announces through Jeremiah that he does not send these other prophets and does not speak through them. Yet they speak as if he did (v. 21). If he had sent them, and if he had spoken through them, they would have turned the people from their evil way and evil doings (v. 22). "I am against those who prophesy lying dreams . . . and who lead my people astray by their lies and their recklessness, when I did not send them or appoint them" (v. 32). The false prophets surely bear a special burden for having led Judah astray, but this burden is not theirs exclusively. Judah has listened to them and not to Jeremiah. It has opted for the false messages of these other prophets and their kings, who claim all is well when all is not well. And because it has chosen other words than the words of the Lord, it too will participate in the judgment God is about to render. Thus says the Lord: "I will surely lift you up and cast you away from my presence, you and the city that I gave to you and your ancestors. And I will bring upon you everlasting disgrace and perpetual shame, which shall not be forgotten" (vv. 39–40).

> "I myself will gather the remnant of my flock out of all the lands where I have driven them, and I will bring them back to their fold, and they shall be fruitful and multiply. . . . I will raise up for David a righteous Branch, and he shall . . . execute justice and righteousness in the land." Jeremiah 23:3, 5.

There is no denying that the central message of chapters 21–23 is one of judgment: judgment against the kings of Judah, judgment against the false prophets, and, by extension, judgment against all those who make the mistake of listening to them and not to the word of the Lord given to them by Jeremiah. But there is another message embedded in these chapters, a message that signals a new word to be announced later in the "Little Book of Consolation" (see unit 10). This new word is a word of hope, here only hinted at, but in a way unique to the book of Jeremiah. It comes as a moment of peace and calmness in the eye of the storm, between the raging winds of

Want to Know More?

About Jehoiakim? See Paul J. Achtemeier, ed., *HarperCollins Bible Dictionary*, rev. ed. (New York: HarperCollins, 1996), 486.

About Zedekiah? See *HarperCollins Bible Dictionary*, 1241.

About Jehoiachin? See *HarperCollins Bible Dictionary*, 485.

About false prophets? See Horst Dietrich Preuss, *Old Testament Theology*, vol. 2 (Louisville, Ky.: Westminster John Knox Press, 1996), 82–86.

About "remnant"? See Preuss, *Old Testament Theology*, 2:271–72.

indictments against the kings on the one side and the indictments against the prophets on the other side. Yahweh speaks: "I myself will gather the remnant of my flock out of all the lands where I have driven them, and I will bring them back to their fold, and they shall be fruitful and multiply. . . . I will raise up for David a righteous Branch, and he shall reign as king and deal wisely, and shall execute justice and righteousness in the land" (23:3, 5). We cannot know with any certainty what this word from the Lord meant to those who first heard it. No doubt it fostered the old dream of a reunited kingdom, a dream of God's people living again in the promised land under a David-like king appointed by Yahweh. But we do know something about what these words have come to mean to Christians. This "righteous Branch" is the Messiah, the one we know as Jesus Christ, and it fosters in us the dream of a new kingdom of God's making where all people dwell together in the justice and righteousness of Christ's Lordship. Such is the hope that nurtures us in times of suffering, pain, and, yes, even judgment.

? Questions for Reflection

1. God is portrayed as a mighty warrior fighting against his own people. Why would God do that? What can we learn from this image? What other images of God serve to balance this one?
2. What role was the king expected to play in the life of Israel and Judah? Was he successful or not? Why?
3. How might today's church leaders be tempted to act like the "false prophets"? What forces might be at work to make such people attractive to modern ears?
4. How do we determine what word is truly the "word of the Lord" and what word is the product of our own dreams?

Jeremiah 29:1–23

A Letter to the Babylonian Exiles

This unit of study concerns fragments of letters by Jeremiah addressed to Jewish exiles in Babylon. While most scholars are unsure about the precise date(s) of these letters, they were most likely written during a period of tension and political unrest in Babylon, sometime after 598 B.C.E. This period of unrest, along with the encouragement of the false prophets seen in unit 8, prompts many of the exiles to expect an imminent return to their homeland. The letter fragments in chapter 29 confirm the message of Jeremiah in chapters 27–28 that the exile will extend over a considerable length of time, at least seventy years (see 29:10).

Chapter 29, like much of the rest of the book of Jeremiah, evidences a lengthy and complicated editorial process. Even so, it provides us with a look at the prophet's pastoral care for the exiles and how he exercised his vocation "over nations and kingdoms" (1:10). Here Jeremiah no doubt surprises the exiles by encouraging them to embrace their time in Babylon as God's time, and also to nurture the hope that perhaps their children or children's children might one day be allowed to return home and rebuild their lives in the promised land. Here we see once more that the pain and suffering of exile is but a prelude to some joyful new work of Yahweh best articulated by the apostle Paul: "suffering produces endurance, and endurance produces character, and character produces hope, and hope does not disappoint us" (Rom. 5:3–5).

Before looking at the text itself, we should note two things about this letter-

"Build houses and live in them; plant gardens and eat what they produce. Take wives and have sons and daughters; take wives for your sons, and give your daughters in marriage, that they may bear sons and daughters; multiply there, and do not decrease." Jeremiah 29:5–6.

writing campaign. First, in antiquity, such letters were not simply passed on in the form in which they were received. They were embellished and interpreted by the messengers who carried them and who read them to the people, a practice that contributed to the long editorial process mentioned above. Second, the exchange of letters between the Jews left in Jerusalem and those deported to Babylon appears to be state sponsored. That is to say, they are carried back and forth by royal envoys (v. 3), most probably in order to ensure the cooperation and payments of tribute from Judah's leaders (see Clements, 171–72).

As we will now see, Jeremiah wants the exiles to understand that their present experience is part of God's plan, so much so that resistance of any kind is tantamount to resisting God (cf. 27:14). Here

Jeremiah's words were written down.

Jeremiah not only counsels the exiles to accept their present situation but he even counsels them to seek the welfare of those who now rule over them (v. 7)! Judah is enmeshed in a strange new world, but it is still God's world. So, even though Judah must suffer the hardships of exile, it still has reason to hope for a better future. Jeremiah attempts to help the nation with this claim and to realize that God's word works until it accomplishes its purpose (see Isa. 55:11).

The Heading of the Letter

Verses 1–3 indicate the author of the letter—Jeremiah; the people to whom the letter is addressed—the elders, priests, and prophets among the exiles, and the people of Judah exiled in Babylon (v. 1); the approximate time of the letter—after King Jeconiah and other leaders, officials, artisans, and tradesmen were deported from Jerusalem (v. 2); and how the letter is sent—by the hand of Elasah under orders from King Zedekiah.

Apparently, there is tension in the Jewish community between those remaining in Jerusalem and those exiled in Babylon. The folks in Jerusalem mistakenly believe that they are somehow special in the sight of God since they are allowed to stay in Jerusalem (cf. chap. 24). Jeremiah, in writing to the exiles, seeks to correct this misunderstanding by affirming the role of the exiles in determining Judah's future. Jeremiah's word to the exiles mirrors God's word to him: they are to "build and plant," living a life of faith even in exile (see v. 5; cf. 1:10).

> "[B]y placing so much emphasis upon the inward and personal aspects of a true knowledge of God Jeremiah's letter established a spiritual foundation for a Jewish existence in the Diaspora (exile). Even though it was not possible in exile to give full expression to what it meant to 'know the Lord,' at the same time it would not be a way of life wholly devoid of such knowledge." R. E. Clements, *Jeremiah*, Interpretation, 173.

Words of Instruction

Jeremiah wants the exiles to make their time in exile count for something. They are to do more than simply mark time. They are given specific instructions: "Build houses and live in them; plant gardens and eat what they produce. Take wives and have sons and daughters; take wives for your sons and give your daughters in marriage, that they may bear sons and daughters" (vv. 5–6). Here, in no uncertain terms, Jeremiah expresses the fact that this exile is going to extend over some period of time and so Judah has to find a way to make the most of it. Jeremiah wants his kinsmen to know that God's promises are not nullified by exile; even there, his people will multiply as they once did in Egypt, thus ensuring some measure of hope for future generations of God's people.

Jeremiah also urges the exiles to do the unthinkable: "seek the welfare of the city where I have sent you into exile, and pray to the LORD on its behalf, for in its welfare you will find your welfare" (v. 7). Here Jeremiah makes it plain that exile is God's doing and thus it is to be embraced and not resisted. Embracing exile means carrying on with the primary work given to them by God, a work that goes all the way back to the covenant with Abraham—to "be a blessing" to the world around them (cf. Gen. 12:2–3). Even in exile, God's people are called to embrace a wider community, to reach out to others with the same love and compassion with which God has reached out to them.

This is still the primary work of God's people. The Bible is clear from the beginning to the end that the individuals and groups called and blessed by God are, in every circumstance, to give themselves in service to the larger community (e.g., Gen. 28:14; 1 Pet. 9:2). People who are blessed are not to hoard their blessing for themselves and/or their own kind of people, but always and everywhere to share those blessings with others, most especially with those who are abused and despised. In the thinking of Old Testament times, it is also clear that when these individuals and groups called and blessed by God do, in fact, work to be a blessing to others, they will continue to benefit from God's good graces. But when they fail to be a blessing to others, they will be cut off from God's good graces and made to suffer the consequences of their sins.

The astonishing aspect of Jeremiah's announcement is that this primary work of God's people is to extend even to one's enemies. This is the hard message of the text now before us, a message that fore-shadows the message of Jesus Christ, who says, "You have heard that it was said, 'You shall love your neighbor and hate your enemy.' But I say to you, Love your enemies and pray for those who persecute you, so that you may be children of your Father in heaven" (Matt. 5:43–45). Just so, God says to Judah: Seek the welfare of Babylon. Pray on Babylon's behalf (v. 7).

Words of Warning

In the next few verses, the attention focuses on the false prophets and their mistaken notion of a quick return from exile. After affirming the kind of long-term commitment Judah is to make to life in Babylon, Jeremiah issues a reminder to his people concerning these other prophets. "Do not let the prophets and the diviners who are among you deceive you, and do not listen to the dreams they dream, for it is a lie that they are prophesying to you" (vv. 8–9). Jeremiah wants the people of Judah to face the reality of exile rather than to focus all of their attention on the illusion of a quick escape proffered by the false prophets.

> **The Exile**
>
> After the destruction of Jerusalem and the temple in 586 B.C., the inhabitants of Judah were split into three groups: 1) those left behind in Judah; 2) those who fled to Egypt and lived in settlements along the Nile; 3) those who were deported by Nebuchadnezzar, roughly 12,000 to 16,000 people. This last group was brought to Babylon and resettled along the banks of the Chebar canal. In an effort to separate themselves from their captors, the exiles began practicing their religious observances with renewed fervor. Having no temple, they gathered together in synagogues (assemblies), and began writing on scrolls many of the oral traditions that had circulated for centuries. When the time came to return to the homeland, those who had learned from the past made their way to Jerusalem, to rebuild the city and renew their covenant with Yahweh. See Celia Brewer Marshall, *A Guide through the Old Testament* (Louisville, Ky.: Westminster John Knox Press, 1989), 114.

"I did not send them, says the LORD" (v. 9), saying, in effect, that those who practice a religion based on a quick fix, an easy out, or a life void of pain and suffering are worshiping something or someone other than Yahweh.

Words of Reassurance

The preceding words focus on the reality of exile and the life God's people are called to live in that time. The focus now shifts to the future, to a time beyond exile. The word God gives to the exiles through the prophet Jeremiah is a word of reassurance, a word that has roots in the covenant promises of old. Sometime after the passing of the present generation, Yahweh will visit the people again in order to fulfill his promise to bring them home to the promised land (v. 10). Once again, Judah is reminded that the underlying will of God is to bring blessing and life to his people, not cursing and death.

Want to Know More?

About the exile? See John Bright, *A History of Israel*, 4th ed. (Louisville, Ky.: Westminster John Knox Press, 2000), chap. 9.

About Ahab? See Paul J. Achtemeier, ed., *HarperCollins Bible Dictionary*, rev. ed. (New York: HarperCollins, 1996), 486.

About Zedekiah? See *HarperCollins Bible Dictionary*, 1241.

About Shemaiah? See *HarperCollins Bible Dictionary*, 1010–11.

This desire to bring blessing and life does not in any way negate or take away the reality of suffering and death; rather, "it moves through, past and beyond judgment to assert Yahweh's final resolve" (Brueggemann, *To Build, To Plant*, 33). "For surely I know the plans I have for you, says the LORD, plans for your welfare and not for harm, to give you a future with hope" (v. 11). The focus here is on the absolute sovereignty of God. As noted before, God is sovereign and free to do whatever God wills to do, and God wills life for God's people, even life beyond exile and death. And because God is sovereign and free, there is nothing that God's people can do or not do to thwart God's plans.

These words of reassurance continue in verses 12–14. Jeremiah announces that this sovereign God who has seemed so distant and so unwilling to help is now ready to hear and answer prayer (v. 12). This sovereign God is now readily accessible to all those who seek in their heart to find him (v. 13). This sovereign God is the same God who rules over Judah and Babylon and all the other nations of the earth, the God who "plucks up and pulls down, destroys and overthrows."

This sovereign God is the one who will "build and plant" (1:10). "I will restore your fortunes and gather you from all the nations and all the places where I have driven you, says the LORD, and I will bring you back to the place from which I sent you into exile" (v. 14). The good news Jeremiah announces in his letter to the exiles is that, when the time is right, God is ready, willing, and able to do a new thing. This is the gift of hope that will enable Judah to endure exile, a gift that points to fresh starts, new beginnings, and new life.

The exile is a time ripe for reflection and repentance, a time for retuning the heart to the will and purpose of God. "By placing so much emphasis upon the inward and spiritual aspects of a true knowledge of God," claims Clements, "Jeremiah's letter establishes a spiritual foundation for a Jewish existence in exile" (173).

Words of Condemnation

The balance of chapter 29 underscores the power of God's word over the nations by condemning the work of Ahab and Zedekiah. They, their kinsfolk, and all the people under their charge in Jerusalem will be consumed by man-made and natural disasters because they still do not listen to God's word, preferring instead to prophesy lies in God's name (vv. 16–23). Likewise, another false prophet, Shemaiah, is condemned because of his opposition to Jeremiah (vv. 29–32).

> "I will pursue them with the sword, with famine, and with pestilence, and will make them a horror to all the kingdoms of the earth . . . because they did not heed my words, says the LORD." Jeremiah 29:18–19.

Thus, chapter 29 ends as it begins—with a large dose of reality. Exile is real. It exists because God wills it. Therefore, it cannot be circumvented by any earthly power of court or temple.

Jeremiah's letter to the exiles captures the heart of his special ministry. It falls to him to announce God's judgment on his people, a judgment that includes the destruction of all things near and dear to them—the destruction of throne and temple, home and family. It is a judgment that will necessitate years of pain, suffering, and death. But it also

> "Exile is real. It exists because God wills it. Therefore, it cannot be circumvented by any earthly power of court or temple."

falls to Jeremiah to announce that such judgment is not the last thing his people will hear or experience from God. Thus, the stage is set for hearing a new word of encouragement and hope, a word we will find in the so-called "Little Book of Consolation" (see unit 10).

 ## Questions for Reflection

1. In what ways do we experience "exile" today? What faith resources are there to help us live through our time of exile? How can we be a source of blessing to others while in exile?
2. Is it realistic to expect a person to pray for, work with, and support one's enemies? How might this be done?
3. Compare and contrast Jeremiah 29:7 and Matthew 5:43–48. What are the implications for us today?
4. How can future promises impact the present? Cite personal and historical examples (such as the hope expressed in the spirituals sung by slaves).

The Little Book of Consolation

While there can be little doubt that the book of Jeremiah is primarily concerned with the downfall of Judah and the apparent breaking of the covenant between Yahweh and his people, it is also a book that dares to speak of Yahweh's power to create new beginnings. It therefore serves as a stimulus for hope for Yahweh's people then and now. There is, as Brueggemann says, "a counter-theme" in the book of Jeremiah, a theme that moves beyond plucking up and tearing down to one of planting and building anew (*To Build, To Plant,* 39). Holladay expands this notion to include the whole of scripture, "theologically, the shape of both the Old Testament and the New Testament suggests that if judgment is God's penultimate word, then God's ultimate word is hope, comfort, and restoration" (*Jeremiah 2,* 201). This ultimate word of God, as noted in previous units, is hinted at in numerous places throughout the book of Jeremiah, but here in chapters 30–31, in the so-called Little Book of Consolation, it comes to full flower.

Chapters 30–31 reveal the steadfast determination of Yahweh to save his people. They reveal the sovereignty and power of Yahweh to rise above the corrupt affairs of court and temple to fulfill his own purposes. They reveal God's ability to create new possibilities for life even in the face of exile, destruction, and death. They reveal that nothing is too hard for Yahweh to do (cf. 32:17, 27). They reveal that God can and will plant what has been plucked up and build what has been pulled down, a work

> "On that day, says the LORD of hosts, I will break the yoke from off his neck, and I will burst his bonds, and strangers shall no more make a servant of him. But they shall serve the LORD their God and David their king, whom I will raise up for them." Jeremiah 30:8–9.

that, generations later, will find new expression and meaning in the resurrection of Jesus Christ.

The primary emphasis of the Little Book of Consolation is "a stunning theological insistence that the historical process is subject to the powerful resolve of God to work a newness, to intrude into old power arrangements and firmly established patterns of reality, to rearrange, reshape, and make new" (Brueggemann, *To Build, To Plant*, 46). It is God's resolve to bring life where there appears to be only death, and this resolve gives birth to a new hope for Judah and for us.

Preamble: Jeremiah 30:1–3

Chapter 30 begins with a vision of rebirth and renewal for Israel and Judah, a vision that originates with Yahweh and is communicated through the prophet Jeremiah, who is instructed to write it in a book (vv. 1–2). This new vision is totally independent of the actions of God's people and their leaders. It involves something that God wills to do on his own because of his great and abiding love for his people. It involves plans for the welfare of God's people, complete with a new future and a new hope (see 29:11). Nevertheless, this new future comes with a price. It is a future that requires the uprooting of prophets, priests, and people, and the dismantling of old regimes and policies of court and temple, the very things now being imposed on Israel and Judah by the divinely appointed armies of Babylon. With these requirements having been met, the stage is finally set for God's new work.

> "We sense in this a drawing out of the Jeremianic message of hope into a more abstract and timeless frame of reference, seeking to hold together the ideas of the divine justice and the divine mercy in respect of God's purpose for Israel." R. E. Clements, *Jeremiah*, Interpretation, 182.

"I will restore the fortunes of my people, Israel and Judah, says the LORD, and I will bring them back to the land that I gave to their ancestors and they shall take possession of it" (v. 3). Israel and Judah will not be scattered in exile forever. Death will not claim all of their children. And the land given to them in covenant with their father Abraham will not be held forever by the Babylonians. God will speak a new word of creation, a word that will one day reconstitute and bless the Jewish nation. To a people down and out for the count, this is indeed radical good news.

Law and Grace: Jeremiah 30:4–11

Next, Jeremiah announces that Yahweh hears the cries of his people—cries of panic, terror, and unrest that heretofore have gone unnoticed (v. 5). It is a time of deep distress—yet help is on the way (v. 7)! The heavy yoke and strong bonds of slavery will be broken, and Israel and Judah will once again be allowed to serve their God and king (vv. 8–9). God's faithfulness to the covenant will turn the people from a state of panic, terror, and unrest to a state of calm assurance.

"Have no fear . . . says the LORD, and do not be dismayed, O Israel; for I am going to save you from far away, and your offspring from the land of their captivity" (v. 10). "I am with you . . . to save you; . . . of you I will not make an end" (v. 11). Here we revisit an old theme commented on earlier in unit 2: Fear not, I am with you. God's presence and power will fulfill this prophecy of salvation. But let us not forget that the gift of salvation is a costly one. "I will chastise you in just measure, and I will by no means leave you unpunished" (v. 11b). Once again, as Clements notes, we are reminded that law and grace are held in creative tension:

> We sense in this a drawing out of the Jeremianic message of hope into a more abstract and timeless frame of reference, seeking to hold together the ideas of the divine justice and the divine mercy in respect of God's purpose for Israel. The experience of exile in Babylon had begun to appear as an ambivalent experience, on the one side affirming the just and punitive action of God to Israel and on the other side revealing a divinely ordained preservation of a faithful remnant of the nation. (182)

This creative tension between law and grace is found throughout the Bible. For Christians, it reaches its creative height in crucifixion and resurrection, proving yet again that suffering and death is not a dead-end street but the way to new life.

Sickness and Healing: Jeremiah 30:12–17

The twin themes of exile and restoration continue in verses 12–17. Judah is once again likened to a child with an incurable disease, a child sick unto death (vv. 12–13). And once again there appears to be no medicine, no doctor, no cure, no balm in Gilead (cf. 8:22). Judah still lives like an unfaithful whore, ignoring her rightful relationship with Yahweh (cf. chap. 3). She has become so soiled that even her lovers forget and neglect her (v. 14). God's judgment for this sick and wayward way of living seems straightforward and familiar: "Why do you cry out over your hurt? Your pain is incurable. Because your guilt is great, because your sins are so numerous, I have done these things to you" (v. 15). Again, Yahweh is protrayed as the prime mover behind Babylon and Judah. Yahweh is the one who invades and scatters. Yahweh is the one who plucks up and pulls down, destroys and overthrows (cf. 1:10).

But judgment is not God's final word. "Therefore," says Yahweh, "all who devour you shall be devoured, . . . those who plunder you shall be plundered, and all who prey on you I will make a prey. For I will restore health to you, and your wounds I will heal" (vv. 16–17). This "therefore" radically changes the direction and flow of the prophecy. It sets us up for a new word from God, a word that brings new possibilities for life to this diseased and wayward people. God declares himself to be the medicine, the doctor, the cure to all that ails Judah. God himself is the faithful and forgiving lover who welcomes Judah into his arms.

We should note that Judah still has not changed. She is just as sick, just as unfaithful as she ever was. The difference is that God has changed! God is no longer the harsh, demanding God, who lawfully and dutifully drops the gavel of judgment on his people. God the great prosecutor has become God the great defender, or as Brueggemann puts it,

---

Jeremiah's Life and Times

c. 650 B.C.E. Jeremiah is born in Anathoth, outside the gates of Jerusalem, to a priestly family.

640–609 Reign of Josiah in Judah.

c. 626 Jeremiah is called to be a prophet.

621 Josiah's reforms (see 2 Kgs. 23:1–25).

612 Nineveh, the capital of Assyria, is destroyed by Babylon.

605–562 Reign of Nebuchadrezzar in Babylonia.

605–597 Reign of Jehoiakim in Judah.

605 Jeremiah predicts the destruction of the temple and declares that opposition to Babylonia is opposition to Yahweh's will. Jehoiakim burns Jeremiah's prophetic scroll. Jeremiah and Baruch go into hiding. Jeremiah writes the Confessions.

597 Nebuchadrezzar places Zedekiah on the throne as a puppet king in Judah.

588 Zedekiah, hoping for support from the new Egyptian pharaoh Hophra, breaks his treaty with Nebuchadrezzar. Jeremiah is imprisoned, thrown into a cistern, and finally placed under house arrest in the palace in Jerusalem.

586 Nebuchadrezzar invades Judah and destroys Jerusalem, including the temple. Zedekiah is blinded and taken in chains to Babylon. The final deportation of the Jews to Babylon occurs; they are resettled by the Chebar River (see 2 Kgs. 25:1–12, Jer. 39:1–14). As Jerusalem falls, Jeremiah purchases the field at Anathoth. His message changes from oracles of doom to oracles of hope, return, and a new covenant. His last letters, written to the exiles in Babylon, are known as the Little Book of Consolation (Jer. 30–31).

"the indignant One has become the compassionate One" *(To Build, To Plant,* 53). Judah and Jerusalem are diseased and past healing, but with God the impossible becomes possible, and what has been unthinkable to this point becomes a future certainty.

The Covenant Reaffirmed: Jeremiah 30:18–22

Verses 18–22 point to the nature of this new work of God. Jerusalem will be rebuilt along with the palace of kings (v. 18). The people of Judah will return giving thanks and making merry, they will multiply and become many, they will be honored by others, and they will produce from their own number a new ruler who will enjoy renewed access to God (vv. 19–21). And capping this new word and work of God is the reaffirmation of a time-honored covenant: "you shall be my people, and I will be your God" (v. 22).

Because of this new and astounding change in God, Israel and Judah have reason to hope. The past is over and done with; the present difficulties are not the final word and work of God. There is a new future on the horizon, a future envisioned and empowered by God, a future that gives rise to new hope.

A New Vision for Israel: Jeremiah 31:2–6

This section of the Little Book of Consolation recalls the fact that Israel's existence as a people is owing to the providence of God. God is the one who calls Israel into being and initiates a relationship with it. God is the one who establishes covenant with Israel. God is the one who guides, sustains, corrects, saves, and loves Israel. "Israel does not and cannot exist in and of itself. It exists as a people only as the outward expression of a decision of divine love" (Clements, 185).

This divine love is the basis for the hope offered in the Little Book of Consolation. This divine love is the one constant in the midst of the many variables of Israel's storied history. "I have loved you with an everlasting love; therefore I have continued my faithfulness to you" (v. 3). Here Yahweh affirms his reliability and his resolve to love his people through this terrible time of judgment. Yahweh's love is put in tension with his judgment; it gives new meaning to it, and it gives Israel reason to hope because it suggests that the future is in no way nullified by present circumstances.

"Again I will build you, and you shall be built, O virgin Israel! Again you shall take your tambourines, and go forth in the dance of the merrymakers. Again you shall plant vineyards on the mountains . . . and shall enjoy the fruit" (vv. 4–5). Here Yahweh affirms his continued interest in creating things. Israel will be "built" again to make music and dance, and to enjoy the fruits of the earth. It will be a time of blessing and abundance, a time that harkens back to Eden before the introduction of sin.

It is a grand and glorious vision, a veritable love feast between God and his people. It is a sweeping vision that touches every aspect of Israel's life. It "holds together theological, socioeconomic, and political dimensions of communal life; everything begins anew" (Brueggemann, *To Build, To Plant*, 60). It is a vision capped off with a gracious invitation: "Come, let us go up to Zion, to the LORD our God" (v. 6).

Back to Zion: Jeremiah 31:7–14

Yahweh's vision for Israel is indeed all-encompassing. It gathers up the whole community, those scattered in exile and those still alive in and around Jerusalem, inviting them all to sing and shout and render praise to God. "Sing aloud with gladness for Jacob, and raise shouts for the chief of the nations; proclaim, give praise, and say, 'Save, O LORD, your people, the remnant of Israel'" (v. 7).

Yahweh's vision is spelled out in some detail. People will be gathered from all parts of the world. Among them will be the most vulnerable of God's people: the blind, the lame, and the pregnant (v. 8). They will join in a great pilgrimage to Zion. They will journey with tears in their eyes because of the consoling comfort of God. They will be nourished with brooks of water and walk securely on the paths that God has laid down for them. They will be treated as firstborn children, inheriting the full benefits of God their father (v. 9).

Yahweh will gather and protect his people as a good shepherd gathers and protects his sheep (v. 10). Yahweh will ransom and redeem his people from the strong hands of their oppressors (v. 11). The people will be so overcome by the goodness of Yahweh that they will sing and dance and make merry (vv. 12–13). They will become glad and joyful people, fully satisfied in the bounty of the Lord (vv. 13–14).

Yahweh's vision brings with it a series of reversals, showing again that, with God, all things are possible. The last and the least will become the first and the greatest. The scattered will be gathered. The lost and enslaved will be found and redeemed. Yahweh will exercise his great power to create a new world. This new world will be grand and glorious, causing Israel to sing and dance and make merry, finally giving God the praise God so richly deserves.

Hope for the Future: Jeremiah 31:15–22

This section of the Little Book of Consolation contains some of the most moving passages in all of the prophetic literature. It speaks to the intensity of Yahweh's love for Israel. Rachel is distraught over the loss of her children. She weeps for them in a way that only a mother can weep. Her grief transcends time, speaking to anyone who has lost a child. God speaks to her, and in his speaking, God does what no human can do—he comforts her with astonishing good news: "Keep your voice from weeping, and your eyes from tears; for there is a reward for your work, . . . there is hope for your future . . . : your children shall come back" (v. 16). Again, the lost are found, the scattered are gathered, and hope is born anew.

Then, after the mother grieves and God intervenes, the lost child speaks. It is the speech we have been waiting for throughout the book of Jeremiah. It is a speech of repentance, in which Israel finally asks for help and acknowledges its sins: "Bring me back, let me come back, for you are the LORD my God. . . . I was ashamed and dismayed because I bore the disgrace of my youth" (vv. 18b-19).

Israel's admission of sin and its desire to come home tugs at the very heart of God. "Is Ephraim my dear son? Is he the child I delight in? . . . I still remember him. Therefore I am deeply moved for him; I will surely have mercy on him" (v. 20). Here is the action we have been waiting for throughout the book of Jeremiah. Here we see God in a different light. Here God replaces the gavel of justice with the hand of mercy, and this mercy inaugurates a whole new future for his children.

This section of the Little Book of Consolation paints God in very human terms. Clements notes that "all significant theological reflection must relate to human existence in its method, since it

> "All significant theological reflection must relate to human existence in its method, since it must learn to understand God in terms of persons, not of things. Human relationships, which are of necessity only a partial and imperfect guide to the nature of God, may nevertheless be the most helpful and significant witnesses to the being of God that we possess." R. E. Clements, *Jeremiah*, Interpretation, 187.

must learn to understand God in terms of persons, not of things. Human relationships . . . may nevertheless be the most helpful and significant witnesses to the being of God that we possess" (187). Just so, God grieves like mother Rachel. God hears the pleas of his children and begins to reminisce about his relationship with them as any parent might do. And, like us in a similar circumstance, God finds his heart strangely warmed and decides that what his children need most in their present situation is not more judgment but mercy.

In his great mercy, God calls Israel home. He instructs Israel to set up road markers, to make guideposts, to consider well the highway in order to find her way back to her cities (v. 21). These "markers" most likely refer to torah, suggesting that the way to this new future is part and parcel to the will and way of God found in the law. God is "creating a new thing on the earth," and his children will be a part of it (v. 22)!

Judah Restored: Jeremiah 31:23–26

This section brings Judah into this new future along with Ephraim (a designation for Israel), thus reaffirming that Israel is one people. This reunited people will raise their collective voices in the sacred liturgies, acknowledging that God is no longer absent, but can be found again in Zion. Judah will be restored in all her splendor. City folk and country folk alike will come to know God's blessing when this new future arrives. They will find themselves satisfied and replenished by the God who calls them home.

Sowing Seeds of Life: Jeremiah 31:27–30

God is about to do a new thing. He is about to sow the house of Israel and the house of Judah with the seed of humans and animals, blessing them with offspring and sustenance (v. 27). He announces that the time of plucking up and breaking down is over and the new time of building and planting has begun (v. 28).

Clements notes that "this careful balancing and interlocking of themes to

"In preserving the record of Jeremiah's prophecies, the unknown scribes and compilers have done so with a view to assisting men and women overtaken by tragedies to face them, to respond courageously to them, and to look in hope beyond them."
R. E. Clements, *Jeremiah*, Interpretation, 3.

make clear the passing of the period of judgment and the coming of the time for renewal and restoration is a significant feature in all the prophetic literature of the Old Testament" (188). Such a juxtaposition places Israel in an in-between time, a time between the death and destruction already experienced and a time of new life anticipated sometime in the future. That is where Israel must live, and it is where we must live even now.

The New Covenant: Jeremiah 31:31–34

"I will make a new covenant with the house of Israel and the house of Judah. . . . I will put my law within them, and I will write it on their hearts; and I will be their God, and they shall be my people" (vv. 31, 33). These are among the best-known verses in all of scripture, and for good reason. Here Yahweh announces a new way of relating to him. No longer will the law, or torah, be imposed on people from the outside; rather, it will be put within people, made a part of them as a gift from God.

> "Yahweh wants more than a knowledge of the law—he wants obedience to the law."

Most scholars agree that these verses do not do away with the old laws given to Moses on Mount Sinai; rather, they give people a new way of knowing and keeping those laws. Yahweh will transform his people and give them hearts to rightly discern and keep his laws. Clements's insights are helpful here: "The concern in the Old Testament passages, in contrast to what emerged later in Christian thinking, was not for a law that could be summarized in certain succinct, fundamental principles. Rather it was for an obedient attitude towards the law. The central attention is upon the willingness to obey the known law, not for the clarification of obscure or conflicting elements within the law" (191). Yahweh wants more than a knowledge of the law—he wants obedience to the law. As we have noted in previous units, Yahweh wants his people to "walk the walk" and not just "talk the talk." This is similar to what

---

The New Covenant

In *To Build, To Plant*, biblical scholar Walter Brueggemann points out four key elements of the new covenant (Jer. 31:33–34):

1. The people will be in solidarity.
2. The people will have a full knowledge of Yahweh.
3. All people will be on equal ground before Yahweh.
4. Yahweh will forgive the sins of the people.

James admonishes in the New Testament: "Be doers of the word, and not merely hearers" (James 1:22).

Brueggemann offers four observations on the nature of the new covenant Yahweh will inaugurate. First, the people will be in solidarity (v. 33). Second, there will be full knowledge of Yahweh, by which he means both the cognitive capacity to recite saving history and a readiness to obey God's commands for justice (v. 34). Third, all people will be on equal ground before Yahweh. No one will lack what is required and no one will be left out of this new relationship with Yahweh. All people will know the salvation story, all will accept the sovereignty of Yahweh, and all will embrace his commands. Fourth, this newness is possible only because Yahweh will break away from a system of rewards and punishments. He will forgive, and that will change everything (*To Build, To Plant*, 71–72). "I will forgive their iniquity, and remember their sin no more" (v. 34).

> "I will be their God, and they shall be my people." Jeremiah 31:33.

It is God's willingness to forgive that becomes the basis of hope for the future. This is the message of God delivered through the prophet Jeremiah, a message that "invites Jews (and belatedly Christians and others) to stand in grateful awe before the miracle of forgiveness, to receive it, and to take from it a new, regenerated life" (Brueggemann, *To Build, To Plant*, 73).

Assurance and Hope: Jeremiah 31:35–40

Verses 35–40 bring the Little Book of Consolation to a close by focusing our attention first on God's providential care of the universe. The message is clear: If God cares enough for his people to give the sun for light, order the moon and stars for light by night, and stir up the seas to roar, then surely he cares enough to preserve and protect his people (vv. 35–36). And if God cares enough to set out the heavens and build the foundations of the earth, then surely he cares enough to look after all the children of Israel (v. 37). Indeed, nothing can break the bonds of love that God has with his people. It is a message that anticipates

> "For I am convinced that neither death, nor life, nor angels, nor rulers, nor things present, nor things to come, nor powers, nor height, nor depth, nor anything else in all creation, will be able to separate us from the love of God in Christ Jesus our Lord." Romans 8:38–39.

what is perhaps the greatest and most hope-filled passage in all of the Bible: "[Nothing] in all creation will be able to separate us from the love of God" (Rom. 8:39). Just so, Jeremiah boldly proclaims that nothing, not even the events of 587 B.C.E., can separate Israel from God's deep and abiding love!

These stirring speeches give rise to a new hope, and for Israel much of that hope concerns Jerusalem. It is fitting, then, that the Little Book of Consolation closes with a word about Zion, the city of God. It will be rebuilt, never again to be uprooted or overthrown (vv. 38, 40b). Though clearly this is poetic hyperbole, it nevertheless points to the important role Jerusalem is to play in God's new future.

Want to Know More?

About the new covenant? See Celia Brewer Marshall, *A Guide through the Old Testament* (Louisville, Ky.: Westminster John Knox Press, 1989), 113–14; Walter Brueggemann, *To Build, To Plant: A Commentary on Jeremiah 26–52* (Grand Rapids: Wm. B. Eerdmans Publishing Co., 1991).

As we have seen throughout this study, it falls to Jeremiah to explain the tragic events in Israel's and Judah's lives. Without a doubt, his prophecies bear witness to the terrible consequences of sin and rebellion, which affect every aspect of life. Even so, there is embedded in this ancient text a clear message of hope, hope for a good and joyous life beyond suffering and death. As Clements notes, "In preserving the record of Jeremiah's prophecies, the unknown scribes and compilers have done so with a view to assisting men and women overtaken by tragedies to face them, to respond courageously to them, and to look in hope beyond them" (3).

Let us then avail ourselves of this assistance, "for whatever was written in former days was written for our instruction, so that by steadfastness and by the encouragement of the scriptures we might have hope" (Rom. 15:4).

Questions for Reflection

1. The text implies that God can and does change his mind. Is there other evidence in the Bible to support this claim? How do you feel about this idea? Are there some things God cannot or will not change?
2. How do you understand God to be the initiator in creating new things, in his relationships with us, and in the act of saving?

3. The text speaks of "road markers" to help find the way home to Zion. What are the road markers for us?

4. Why is this an "in-between time"? How are we to live in this time? What is our common calling, our role, in God's unfolding work of salvation?

Bibliography

Bright, John. *Jeremiah*. New York: Doubleday, 1965.

Brueggemann, Walter. *To Build, To Plant: A Commentary on Jeremiah 26–52*. Grand Rapids: Wm. B. Eerdmans Publishing Co., 1991.

———. *To Pluck Up, To Tear Down: A Commentary on the Book of Jeremiah 1–25*. Grand Rapids: Wm. B. Eerdmans Publishing Co., 1988.

Carroll, R. P. *From Chaos to Covenant*. London: SCM Press, 1981.

———. *Jeremiah*. Sheffield: JSOT Press, 1989.

Clements, R. E. *Jeremiah*. Interpretation: A Bible Commentary for Teaching and Preaching. Atlanta: John Knox Press, 1988.

Diamond, A. R. *The Confessions of Jeremiah in Context*. Sheffield: JSOT Press, 1987.

Diamond, A. R., Kathleen O' Connor, and Louis Stulmann, eds. *Troubling Jeremiah*. Sheffield: JSOT Press, 1999.

Holladay, William L. *Jeremiah 1: A Commentary on the Book of the Prophet Jeremiah, Chapters 1–25*. Philadelphia: Fortress Press, 1986.

———. *Jeremiah 2: A Commentary on the Book of the Prophet Jeremiah, Chapters 26–52*. Minneapolis: Fortress Press, 1989.

Janzen, John Gerald. *Studies in the Text of Jeremiah*. Cambridge, Mass.: Harvard University Press, 1973.

Kierkegaard, Sören. *The Sickness unto Death*. Princeton, N.J.: Princeton University Press, 1980.

McKane, William. *A Critical/Exegetical Commentary on Jeremiah*. Edinburgh: T. & T. Clark, 1986.

McKeating, Henry. *The Book of Jeremiah*. Petersborough, England: Epworth, 1999.

O'Connor, Kathleen M. *The Confessions of Jeremiah: Their Interpretation and Their Role in Chapters 1–25*. Atlanta: Scholars Press, 1984.

Polk, Timothy. *The Prophetic Persona*. Sheffield: JSOT Press, 1984.

Rowley, H. H. *The Early Prophecies of Jeremiah in Their Setting*. Manchester: John Rylands Library, 1962.

Stulmann, Louis. *Order amid Chaos*. Sheffield: JSOT Press, 1998.

Interpretation Bible Studies
Leader's Guide

Interpretation Bible Studies (IBS), for adults and older youth, are flexible, attractive, easy-to-use, and filled with solid information about the Bible. IBS helps Christians discover the guidance and power of the scriptures for living today. Perhaps you are leading a church school class, a midweek Bible study group, or a youth group meeting, or simply using this in your own personal study. Whatever the setting may be, we hope you find this *Leader's Guide* helpful. Since every context and group is different, this *Leader's Guide* does not presume to tell you how to structure Bible study for your situation. Instead, the *Leader's Guide* seeks to offer choices—a number of helpful suggestions for leading a successful Bible study using IBS.

> "The church that no longer hears the essential message of the Scriptures soon ceases to understand what it is for and is open to be captured by the dominant religious philosophy of the moment."—James D. Smart, *The Strange Silence of the Bible in the Church: A Study in Hermeneutics* (Philadelphia: Westminster Press, 1970), 10.

How Should I Teach IBS?

1. Explore the Format

There is a wealth of information in IBS, perhaps more than you can use in one session. In this case, more is better. IBS has been designed to give you a well-stocked buffet of content and teachable insights. Pick and choose what suits your group's needs. Perhaps you will want to split units into two or more sessions, or combine units into a single session. Perhaps you will decide to use only a portion of a unit and then move on to the next unit. *There is not a structured theme or teaching focus to each unit that must be followed for IBS to be used.* Rather, IBS offers the flexibility to adjust to whatever suits your context.

> "The more we bring to the Bible, the more we get from the Bible." —William Barclay, *A Beginner's Guide to the New Testament* (Louisville, Ky.: Westminster John Knox Press, 1995), vii.

A recent survey of both professional and volunteer church educators revealed that their number one concern was that Bible study materials be teacher-friendly. IBS is indeed teacher-friendly in two important ways. First, since IBS provides abundant content and a flexible design, teachers can shape the lessons creatively, responding to the needs of the group and employing a wide variety of teaching methods. Second, those who wish more specific suggestions for planning the sessions can find them at the Westminster John Knox Press Web site (**www.wjkbooks.com**). Here, you can access a study guide with teaching suggestions for each IBS unit as well as helpful quotations, selections from Bible dictionaries and encyclopedias, and other teaching helps.

IBS is not only teacher-friendly, it is also discussion-friendly. Given the opportunity, most adults and young people relish the chance to talk about the kind of issues raised in IBS. The secret, then, is to determine what works with your group, what will get them to talk. Several good methods for stimulating discussion are presented in this *Leader's Guide*, and once you learn your group, you can apply one of these methods and get the group discussing the Bible and its relevance in their lives.

The format of every IBS unit consists of several features:

a. Body of the Unit. This is the main content, consisting of interesting and informative commentary on the passage and scholarly insight into the biblical text and its significance for Christians today.

b. Sidebars. These are boxes that appear scattered throughout the body of the unit, with maps, photos, quotations, and intriguing ideas. Some sidebars can be identified quickly by a symbol, or icon, that helps the reader know what type of information can be found in that sidebar. There are icons for illustrations, key terms, pertinent quotes, and more.

c. Want to Know More? Each unit includes a "Want to Know More?" section that guides learners who wish to dig deeper and consult other resources. If your church library does not have the resources mentioned, you can look up the information in other standard Bible dictionaries, encyclopedias, and handbooks, or you can find much of this information at the Westminster John Knox Press Web site (see last page of this Guide).

d. Questions for Reflection. The unit ends with questions to help the learners think more deeply about the biblical passage and its pertinence for today. These questions are provided as examples only, and teachers are encouraged both to develop their own list of questions and to gather questions from the group. These discussion questions do not usually have specific "correct" answers. Again, the

> "The trick is to make the Bible our book."— Duncan S. Ferguson, *Bible Basics: Mastering the Content of the Bible* (Louisville, Ky.: Westminster John Knox Press, 1995), 3.

flexibility of IBS allows you to use these questions at the end of the group time, at the beginning, interspersed throughout, or not at all.

2. Select a Teaching Method

Here are ten suggestions. The format of IBS allows you to choose what direction you will take as you plan to teach. Only you will know how your lesson should best be designed for your group. Some adult groups prefer the lecture method, while others prefer a high level of free-ranging discussion. Many youth groups like interaction, activity, the use of music, and the chance to talk about their own experiences and feelings. Here is a list of a few possible approaches. Let your own creativity add to the list!

a. Let's Talk about What We've Learned. In this approach, all group members are requested to read the scripture passage and the IBS unit before the group meets. Ask the group members to make notes about the main issues, concerns, and questions they see in the passage. When the group meets, these notes are collected, shared and discussed. This method depends, of course, on the group's willingness to do some "homework."

b. What Do We Want and Need to Know? This approach begins by having the whole group read the scripture passage together. Then, drawing from your study of the IBS, you, as the teacher, write on a board or flip chart two lists:

(1) Things we should know to better understand this passage (content information related to the passage, for example, historical insights about political contexts, geographical landmarks, economic nuances, etc.), and

(2) Four or five "important issues we should talk about regarding this passage" (with implications for today—how the issues in the biblical context continue into today, for example, issues of idolatry or fear).

"Although small groups can meet for many purposes and draw upon many different resources, the one resource which has shaped the life of the Church more than any other throughout its long history has been the Bible."—Roberta Hestenes, *Using the Bible in Groups* (Philadelphia: Westminster Press, 1983), 14.

Allow the group to add to either list, if they wish, and use the lists to lead into a time of learning, reflection, and discussion. This approach is suitable for those settings where there is little or no advanced preparation by the students.

c. Hunting and Gathering. Start the unit by having the group read the scripture passage together. Then divide the group into smaller clusters (perhaps having as few as one person), each with a different assignment. Some clusters can discuss one or more of the "Questions for Reflection." Others can look up key terms or people in a Bible dictionary or track down other biblical references found in the body of the unit. After the small clusters have had time to complete their tasks, gather the entire group again and lead them through the study material, allowing each cluster to contribute what it learned.

d. From Question Mark to Exclamation Point. This approach begins with contemporary questions and then moves to the biblical content as a response to those questions. One way to do this is for you to ask the group, at the beginning of the class, a rephrased version of one or more of the "Questions for Reflection" at the end of the study unit. For example, one of the questions at the end of the unit on Exodus 3:1–4:17 in the IBS *Exodus* volume reads,

Moses raised four protests, or objections, to God's call. Contemporary people also raise objections to God's call. In what ways are these similar to Moses' protests? In what ways are they different?

This question assumes familiarity with the biblical passage about Moses, so the question would not work well before the group has explored the passage. However, try rephrasing this question as an opening exercise; for example:

Here is a thought experiment: Let's assume that God, who called people in the Bible to do daring and risky things, still calls people today to tasks of faith and courage. In the Bible, God called Moses from a burning bush and called Isaiah in a moment of ecstatic worship in the Temple. How do you think God's call is experienced by people today? Where do you see evidence of people saying "yes" to God's call? When people say "no" or raise an objection to God's call, what reasons do they give (to themselves, to God)?

Posing this or a similar question at the beginning will generate discussion and raise important issues, and then it can lead the group into an exploration of the biblical passage as a resource for thinking even more deeply about these questions.

e. Let's Go to the Library. From your church library, your pastor's library, or other sources, gather several good commentaries on the book of the Bible you are studying. Among the trustworthy commentaries are those in the Interpretation studies (John Knox Press) and the Westminster Bible Companion series (Westminster John Knox Press). Divide your groups into smaller clusters and give one commentary to each cluster (one or more of the clusters can be given the IBS volume instead of a full-length commentary). Ask each cluster to read the biblical passage you are studying and then to read the section of the commentary that covers that passage (if your group is large, you may want to make photocopies of the commentary material with proper permission, of course). The task of each cluster is to name the two or three most important insights they discover about the biblical passage by reading and talking together about the commentary material. When you reassemble the larger group to share these insights, your group will gain not only a variety of insights about the passage but also a sense that differing views of the same text are par for the course in biblical interpretation.

f. Working Creatively Together. Begin with a creative group task, tied to the main thrust of the study. For example, if the study is on the Ten Commandments, a parable, or a psalm, have the group rewrite the Ten Commandments, the parable, or the psalm in contemporary language. If the passage is an epistle, have the group write a letter to their own congregation. Or if the study is a narrative, have the group role-play the characters in the story or write a page describing the story from the point of view of one of the characters. After completion of the task, read and discuss the biblical passage, asking for interpretations and applications from the group and tying in IBS material as it fits the flow of the discussion.

g. Singing Our Faith. Begin the session by singing (or reading) together a hymn that alludes to the biblical passage being studied (or to the theological themes in the passage). For example, if you are studying the unit from the IBS volume on Psalm 121, you can sing "I to the Hills Will Lift My Eyes," "Sing Praise to God, Who Reigns Above," or another hymn based on Psalm 121. Let the group reflect on the thoughts and feelings evoked by the hymn, then move to the biblical passage, allowing the biblical text and the IBS material to underscore, clarify, refine, and deepen the discussion stimulated by the hymn. If you are ambitious, you may ask the group to write a new hymn at the end of the study! (Many hymnals have indexes in the back or companion volumes that help the user match hymns to scripture passages or topics.)

h. Fill in the Blanks. In order to help the learners focus on the content of the biblical passage, at the beginning of the session ask each member of the group to read the biblical passage and fill out a brief questionnaire about the details of the passage (provide a copy for each learner or write the questions on the board). For example, if you are studying the unit in the IBS *Matthew* volume on Matthew 22:1–14, the questionnaire could include questions such as the following:

—In this story, Jesus compares the kingdom of heaven to what?
—List the various responses of those who were invited to the king's banquet but who did not come.
—When his invitation was rejected, how did the king feel? What did the king do?
—In the second part of the story, when the king saw a man at the banquet without a wedding garment, what did the king say? What did the man say? What did the king do?
—What is the saying found at the end of this story?

Gather the group's responses to the questions and perhaps encourage discussion. Then lead the group through the IBS material helping the learners to understand the meanings of these details and the significance of the passage for today. Feeling creative? Instead of a fill-in-the-blanks questionnaire, create a crossword puzzle from names and words in the biblical passage.

i. Get the Picture. In this approach, stimulate group discussion by incorporating a painting, photograph, or other visual object into the lesson. You can begin by having the group examine and comment on this visual or you can introduce the visual later in the lesson—it depends on the object used. If, for example, you are studying the unit Exodus 3:1–4:17 in the IBS *Exodus* volume, you may want to view Paul Koli's very colorful painting *The Burning Bush*. Two sources for this painting are *The Bible through Asian Eyes,* edited by Masao Takenaka and Ron O'Grady (National City, Calif.: Pace Publishing Co., 1991), and *Imaging the Word: An Arts and Lectionary Resource,* vol. 3, edited by Susan A. Blain (Cleveland: United Church Press, 1996).

j. Now Hear This. Especially if your class is large, you may want to use the lecture method. As the teacher, you prepare a presentation on the biblical passage, using as many resources as you have available plus your own experience, but following the content of the IBS unit as a guide. You can make the lecture even more lively by asking the learners at various points along the way to refer to the visuals and quotes found in the "sidebars." A place can be made for questions (like the ones at the end of the unit)—either at the close of the lecture or at strategic points along the way.

> "It is . . . important to call a Bible study group back to what the text being discussed actually says, especially when an individual has gotten off on some tangent."—Richard Robert Osmer, *Teaching for Faith: A Guide for Teachers of Adult Classes* (Louisville, Ky.: Westminster John Knox Press, 1992), 71.

3. Keep These Teaching Tips in Mind

There are no surefire guarantees for a teaching success. However, the following suggestions can increase the chances for a successful study:

a. Always Know Where the Group Is Headed. Take ample time beforehand to prepare the material. Know the main points of the study, and know the destination. Be flexible, and encourage discussion, but don't lose sight of where you are headed.

b. Ask Good Questions; Don't Be Afraid of Silence. Ideally, a discussion blossoms spontaneously from the reading of the scripture. But more often than not, a discussion must be drawn from the group members by a series of well-chosen questions. After asking each question, give the group members time to answer. Let them think, and don't be threatened by a season of silence. Don't feel that every question must have an answer, and that as leader, you must supply every answer. Facilitate discussion by getting the group members to cooperate with each other. Sometimes the original question can be restated. Sometimes it is helpful to ask a follow-up question like "What makes this a hard question to answer?"

Ask questions that encourage explanatory answers. Try to avoid questions that can be answered simply "Yes" or "No." Rather than asking, "Do you think Moses was frightened by the burning bush?" ask, "What do you think Moses was feeling and experiencing as he stood before the burning bush?" If group members answer with just one word, ask a follow-up question like "Why do you think this is so?" Ask questions about their feelings and opinions, mixed within questions about facts or details. Repeat their responses or restate their response to reinforce their contributions to the group.

> "Studies of learning reveal that while people remember approximately 10% of what they hear, they remember up to 90% of what they say. Therefore, to increase the amount of learning that occurs, increase the amount of talking about the Bible which each member does."—Roberta Hestenes, *Using the Bible in Groups* (Philadelphia: Westminster Press, 1983), 17.

Most studies can generate discussion by asking open-ended questions. Depending on the group, several types of questions can work. Some groups will respond well to content questions that can be answered from reading the IBS comments or the biblical passage. Others will respond well to questions about feelings or thoughts. Still others will respond to questions that challenge them to new thoughts or that may not have exact answers. Be sensitive to the group's dynamic in choosing questions.

Some suggested questions are: What is the point of the passage? Who are the main characters? Where is the tension in the story? Why does it say (this) _____, and not (that) _____? What raises questions for you? What terms need defining? What are the new ideas? What doesn't make sense? What bothers or troubles you about this passage? What keeps you from living the truth of this passage?

c. Don't Settle for the Ordinary. There is nothing like a surprise. Think of special or unique ways to present the ideas of the study. Upset the applecart of the ordinary. Even though the passage may be familiar, look for ways to introduce suspense. Remember that a little mystery can capture the imagination. Change your routine.

Along with the element of surprise, humor can open up a discussion. Don't be afraid to laugh. A well-chosen joke or cartoon may present the central theme in a way that a lecture would have stymied.

Sometimes a passage is too familiar. No one speaks up because everyone feels that all that could be said has been said. Choose an unfamiliar translation from which to read, or if the passage is from a Gospel, compare the story across two or more Gospels and note differences. It is amazing what insights can be drawn from seeing something strange in what was thought to be familiar.

d. Feel free to Supplement the IBS Resources with Other Material. Consult other commentaries to resources. Tie in current events with the lesson. Scour newspapers or magazines for stories that touch on the issues of the study. Sometimes the lyrics of a song, or a section of prose from a well-written novel will be just the right seasoning for the study.

e. And Don't Forget to Check the Web. You can download a free study guide from our Web site (**www.wjkbooks.com**). Each study guide includes several possibilities for applying the teaching methods suggested above for individual IBS units.

f. Stay Close to the Biblical Text. Don't forget that the goal is to learn the Bible. Return to the text again and again. Avoid making the mistake of reading the passage only at the beginning of the study, and then wandering away to comments on top of comments from that point on. Trust in the power

> "The Bible is literature, but it is much more than literature. It is the holy book of Jews and Christians, who find there a manifestation of God's presence." —Kathleen Norris, *The Psalms* (New York: Riverhead Books, 1997), xxii.

and presence of the Holy Spirit to use the truths of the passage to work within the lives of the study participants.

What If Am Using IBS in Personal Bible Study?

If you are using IBS in your personal Bible study, you can experiment and explore a variety of ways. You may choose to read straight through the study without giving any attention to the sidebars or other features. Or you may find yourself interested in a question or unfamiliar with a key term, and you can allow the sidebars "Want to

Know More?" and "Questions for Reflection" to lead you into deeper learning on these issues. Perhaps you will want to have a few commentaries or a Bible dictionary available to pursue what interests you. As was suggested in one of the teaching methods above, you may want to begin with the questions at the end, and then read the Bible passage followed by the IBS material. Trust the IBS resources to provide good and helpful information, and then follow your interests!

 Want to Know More?

About leading Bible study groups? See Roberta Hestenes, *Using the Bible in Groups* (Philadelphia: Westminster Press, 1983).

About basic Bible content? See Duncan S. Ferguson, *Bible Basics: Mastering the Content of the Bible* (Louisville, Ky.: Westminster John Knox Press, 1995); William M. Ramsay, *The Westminster Guide to the Books of the Bible* (Louisville, Ky.: Westminster John Knox Press, 1994).

About the development of the Bible? See John Barton, *How the Bible Came to Be* (Louisville, Ky.: Westminster John Knox Press, 1997).

About the meaning of difficult terms? See Donald K. McKim, *Westminster Dictionary of Theological Terms* (Louisville, Ky.: Westminster John Knox Press, 1996); Paul J. Achtemeier, *Harper's Bible Dictionary* (San Francisco: Harper & Row, 1985).

To download a free IBS study guide,
visit our Web site at
www.wjkbooks.com.